FOX TRAPPING

A Book of Instruction Telling How to Trap, Snare, Poison and Shoot A Valuable Book for Trappers

by Arthur Robert Harding

Edited by Arthur Robert Harding

Originally published in 1906.

CONTENTS:

I General Information

II. Baits and Scents

III. Foxes and Odor

IV. Chaff Method, Scent

V. Traps and Hints

VI. All Round Land Set

VII. Snow Set

VIII. Trapping Red Fox

IX. Red and Grey

X. Wire and Twine Snare

XI. Trap, Snare, Shooting and Poison

XII. My First Fox

XIII. Tennessee Trapper's Method

XIV. Many Good Methods

XV. Fred and the Old Trapper

XVI. Experienced Trapper's Tricks

XVII. Reynard Outwitted

XVIII. Fox Shooting

XIX. A Shrewd Fox

XX. Still Hunting The Fox

XXI. Fox Ranches

XXII. Steel Traps

INTRODUCTORY.

If all the methods as given in this book had been studied out by one man and he began trapping when Columbus discovered America, more than four hundred years ago, he would not be half completed.

The methods given on the following pages are principally taken from articles published in the H-T-T, and as the writers give their own most successful methods, the trapper of little experience with fox will find them of great value.

Their articles are from all parts of America, so that trappers from any section will find a method or methods that can be used. The red fox is the one most sets describe, yet what is a good method for one species is apt to be for others.

    A. R. HARDING.

FOX TRAPPING

CHAPTER I.

GENERAL INFORMATION.

Foxes are found in all parts of America, but probably most numerous in the New England States and parts of Canada. The range of the red is from Virginia to Alaska; grey, Southern and Southwestern States; cross, Northern New Jersey to Manitoba; black, Alaska, and the territories several hundred miles to the South and East; swift, the prairies or Great Plains; white and blue, the Arctic Regions.

While their fur has been one of value for many, many years, and they have been hunted, trapped and snared, yet their numbers are holding up remarkably well owing to their shrewdness. While many tricks are claimed for foxes that they never did, yet they are very cunning animals and also fleet on foot.

In hilly and mountainous countries they travel much on the highest ground, and have regular "crossings," where the experienced hunter or trapper often makes a kill or catch.

Foxes are carnivorous--living on flesh. Their principal food consists of rabbits, squirrels, mice, birds, bugs, eggs, etc. In some places where the food named is not plenty they visit creeks, lakes and ponds hunting crabs and fish. While they prefer fresh meat, they take stale and even decayed meats in severe weather.

Most wild animals can be attracted a short distance by "scent" or "decoy," and the fox is one of them. Several good recipts for scent are given, but if there are no foxes in your neighborhood you can use all the "scents" and "decoys" you wish on a hundred traps all season without making a catch. There is no "decoy" that will attract a fox a mile, but there are some that are good. That many of the writers made good catches is bourn out by the various photographs, and in some instances by personal visits by the author to the trapper.

Foxes should not be trapped or shot until cold weather. In the states bordering on Canada about November 1st, while to the north they become prime sooner, while to the south they do not become prime until later.

The pelt should be cased, that is skinned without ripping, and drawn upon a board. Several tacks or small nails can be used to hold the skin in place. Leave on the board only two to five days, according to the weather. When removed, turn fur side out. In drying, keep in a cool shady place and free from smoke. The number caught and killed annually is not known, but of the various kinds--red, grey, cross, white, etc.--it is several hundred thousand.

The following letters cover trapping and snaring pretty thoroughly, and all who read carefully and set their traps according to directions (if there are any foxes) will probably be successful. While the No. 2 Newhouse, which is a double spring, is known as the fox trap, the No. 1 1/2 single spring will hold the animal. We have known of several instances where fine "reds" were caught in a No. 1 trap. In those instances, however, the trap was fastened to a loose brush and every time the fox made a lunge the brush gave. In using the larger size, we advise using a brush or clog that will give with every pull or jump of the fox. Traps should be visited every other day, if possible, but never go only near enough to see that nothing has been disturbed.

Owing to the wide distribution of the fox and the fact that they often have crossings near buildings so that their tracks are seen, etc., makes many inexperienced trappers think the number of animals larger than it really is. The fact that foxes travel during the coldest weather as well as any other time, gives the trapper an opportunity to show his skill when such animals as bear, coon, skunk, opossum and muskrat are "denned up." Fox skins at such times are at their best.

As mentioned elsewhere, the greater per cent of the methods published in this book are taken from the Hunter-Trader-Trapper, an illustrated monthly magazine, of Columbus, Ohio, devoted to Hunting, trapping and raw furs. New trapping methods are constantly being published in that magazine, as experienced trappers from all parts of North America read and write for it.

CHAPTER II.

BAITS AND SCENTS.

I prefer cat or muskrat for bait, says G. W. Asha. Cut it in pieces as large as an egg, place it in a perfectly clean can, zinc, screw cover, place it in the sun, allowing the bait to taint. This must be done in July or August, or can be done about two weeks before using. In regard to using scents, many don't believe scent is a help to trappers, but I'm one that believes in scent, because if there's a heavy rain storm it takes the scent from the bait. If a little scent is added, your bait is fresh again. Even heavy frosts have the same effect in this case. You have seen advertisements saying that scents will call an animal a mile. Don't take any stock in it, because any animal can't smell at the most only a few hundred feet away if the wind is right, not half as far if the wind is not right.

If any of you are beginners trapping fox, scent is a great help, if you happen to tuck anything around the trap that have effect, if a little scent is added. A fox can smell only one thing at a time. If the scent is stronger than human scent, they will not smell the human scent. Too many accidents in this way have their effect because the fox is a forest animal in existence. I use for fall trapping the fox pure skunk glands and pure strained honey (not sugar fed honey) but clover or flower honey. Winter scent, pure matrix from the female fox taken in the running season during the heat, a little muskrat musk and pure strained honey. This scent attracts the male fox and is the strongest scent in existence.

Here is a first class fox decoy which can be made very easily, write Irving Brown, of Vermont. Take one half pint of skunk oil and the musk glands of a muskrat and one scent bag of a skunk, and you have the celebrated scent of Schofield, one of the first water set fox trappers in the East. This should be made in spring, but it is all right made at any time. It is not the best scent, however, but it is a most excellent one.

Here is the secret of the best and it is hard to prepare because you cannot get the female fox in the running season, which is February or March, in this climate very easily. Take the matrix of a female fox taken in the running season or, in other words, cut out the entire sexual organs and place them in a pint of alcohol, and the result will be the best scent ever made. Some do not use alcohol but salt the matrix. This is the scent you will buy the secret for $5.00, and you will be told that foxes are just crazy to get it. This is in a measure true, but a red fox will not step into a trap unless you use care in setting it, with any kind of scent. I don't care how frantic a fox is to get at the bait. They don't commit suicide if they know it.

There are many other ways to prepare for both mink and fox, all of them possessing merit, but my aim is to give the best, not those which are no use to the trapper. The more simple, as a rule, are the best. Some trappers are opposed to the use of scent, but you will find that man far behind others. The capture of fur bearing animals has become a science, as mink and fox become more wary so does man become more skillful in overcoming their shyness. We hear lots of secrets that were learned of the Indians. No doubt they had some good ones too, but the white trapper in the same place will outdistance any Indian I have ever seen or heard of. My experience among those people is that they are too lazy to use the care that a white man will use in either setting traps or stretching skins.

I have had a fox get into my snowshoes tracks and follow a long way because it was better traveling, says M. H. McAllister. Now that shows he was not afraid of human scent. Now about iron. How often does a fox go through a wire fence, or go near an old sugar house where there are iron gates? That shows he is not afraid of scent of iron.

Once there was an old trapper here, and the young men wanted him to show them how to set a fox trap, and he told them he would. So he got them out to show them how, and this is what he told them: "Remove all suspicion and lay a great temptation." Well, there it is. Now, in order to remove all suspicion you must remove all things that are not natural. A man's tracks and where he has been digging around with a spade or with his hands are not natural around a spring, are they? No. Well then, there is where the human scent question comes in. By instinct he is shown that man is his enemy, and when a man has pawed the bait over he uses his sense and knows that there is danger, for it is not natural.

Now I have a question at hand. In one place he is not afraid and around the trap he is afraid. Now, how does he know when to be afraid or not? I think because when he sees a piece of bait in a new place it is not natural. Once last winter I knew where there was a dead horse and I used to go by it, and one day my brother was with me and of course he knew I could get a fox there, so to please him I set a trap, and not another fox came near. Well I smoked that trap, boiled it in hemlock and then smeared it with tallow, but the fox knew and never came within ten feet of it again, when they were coming every night before. When I went by there before I set my trap I left as much scent as after, and how could he tell when there was a foot of snow blown there by the wind after I set my trap.

Now they don't appear to be afraid of human scent or iron in some places and around a trap they are, so now why should they know where to be shy? Well, because it may be in an unnatural place, unless it is instinct or good sharp sense. As for scent, I know that rotten eggs and onions are not natural, although the matrix of the female fox in the running season is very good. Also such as skunk or muskrat scent or fish, as it smells rotten and makes a strong smell.

One word to the novice fox trapper, and I will leave space for something more valuable. You must make things look natural around the spring and smell natural, and put before them the food that God has provided for them, and you will have success by placing the trap in the mud of the spring, and putting a sod on the pan of the trap that has not been handled by the hand of a human being.

CHAPTER III.

FOXES AND ODOR.

Last winter I could not trap much because the river along which I do my trapping and the woods all around were full of lumbermen, and I was afraid my traps would be stolen. I did a little experimenting on foxes in their relations to the odor of man and iron, says Omer Carmerk, of Quebec.

The results of my experiences confirmed my previous observation that foxes are not afraid of the odor of iron, neither of the odor of man, but mighty suspicious of a bait connected with both odors. I made a trail about two miles long, scattered about it pieces of meat, chicken, rabbit, cheese, etc. I dragged a dead chicken, but I set no trap. Prior to my baiting the trail foxes were crossing it and following it without hesitation, but after I had put out the bait not a fox had ventured to cross that trail again.

One day I saw where a fox had come near the trail, stopped, wheeled about and bounded off like a frightened deer. Another day, a fox tried to cross it at three different places but could not summon up enough courage, and at last, by making a long detour he crossed it at a place where there was no bait, not 20 yards from my cabin. One time a fox walked parallel to the trail several rods, then came nearer to it, stopped and turned back at full speed. The same foxes which were so afraid of my trail were going every night on the public road to eat horses.

I will now relate one instance showing that the foxes smell traps. One day I chopped a chicken on a log. I threw the big pieces in the middle of three traps I had set the week before and left many small pieces on the log. The day after the snow around and on the log was all tramped down by foxes. One fox walked towards the big piece of meat, and when about two inches from a trap he stopped and turned back. I have no doubt he smelled the trap. When the traps are in the snow or wet ground the oxidation of iron produces a peculiar odor noticeable even to the human nostrils.

One day I was going to look at a trap in a swamp road. My dog was trotting ahead of me, and when about ten feet from the trap he stopped and turned around. He detected the odor of the trap for he had not seen me set it, and he had good reasons to avoid it because when young he had often been pinched.

Perhaps my experience does not harmonize with that of other trappers, but the ways of foxes as well as other animals are much influenced by their surroundings. I have observed that foxes frequenting the neighborhood of farms are less suspicious than those living in the deep woods.

For years, says a Southern trapper, I have invariably caught my fox, whether in a path, water or bait set; but can I swear my success is attributable to my extreme precaution? I always smoke traps to kill the smell of iron then handle them and everything around the setting with gloves, to erase human scent.

I have found the summer and early fall months the best time to locate the haunts of the fox, as they are sure to use the same territory in the winter season. While on one of my recent investigating tours, a few days after a rain, I observed some facts that will be interesting.

I struck an old road running through a farm, and readily noticed some fox tracks. Naturally I followed on and found they led under a wheat harvester, which had been recently left in the road and on under an iron gate, into the pasture beyond. All know that a harvester is largely constructed of iron and steel. Now if the fox is so afraid of this metal, as is supposed, does it seem reasonable that he would walk under such a mass of iron, or under an iron gate?

In fox trapping the smoking and smearing process is advocated as well as the handling with gloves and concealing under the ground. In the light of my observations, are all these precautions absolutely necessary? On this same trip, in question, I noticed a fox track, and as usual followed it. To my surprise the animal went within a hair's breadth of a plow, passing right on, seemingly not either to care for red paint or iron construction.

How is it, fox trappers? Does the iron and steel used in farm implements differ from that used in steel traps, so that the latter must be handled with such care as is advocated by many of the trapper's profession? Or is it the covering of the trap with earth that arouses suspicion?

A red or grey fox will cross through or under a wire fence over the public highway at night, although the roads are continually traversed by the iron bound shoes of the horse. Even the tracks of man are visible here yet we, when trapping, brush out our tracks with great care.

I have known a fox to follow where a plow has been dragged and have seen his tracks in the iron marked groove, just made by the locked wheel of a wagon.

Considering these facts, does it seem possible that the fox has so great an antipathy to iron and to the human scent as supposed? (We believe that the conditions under which these are found have much to do with the foxes shrewdness. A wagon wheel or binder never caught a fox, but the scent coming from a trap--well that is different. Coming down to this would appear that the fox has some reasoning power or intellect.--Editor.)

CHAPTER IV.

CHAFF METHOD, SCENT.

Get some chaff, a bushel will do, and put it out in some good place where there are foxes, writes a Maine trapper, J. F. Miller. Put some small pieces of meat in the chaff, (skunk, muskrat or cat is good), and take a shingle and pound the bed down solid all over. Don't have any soft place in the bed, and don't handle any of the chaff with bare hands, or the bait either. Leave it in this shape until you go on, then get your trap ready to set, but you want your trap clean and free from rust, and this is a good way to do. Scrape with an old knife, then use a clean pan and boil in clean water for twenty minutes, and no fox can smell your trap. Set in edge of bed and cover in good shape, and make it look as natural as possible, and don't walk all around in snow, stand in one place and walk in same tracks when you visit this place, and don't go only every other day.

Now I will tell you of a good way to make a scent that will draw a fox to a trap. It will draw a fox a number of yards, but it will not draw them one mile or one half mile, and I doubt if it will one fourth mile, or any other scent that was ever made or ever will be. That is my idea of scents, but I know that they are good to draw animals to traps; they are like methods, some are better than others. This is not the best, but it is good. Take a cat, skunk and muskrat in April, dress them and chop them up fine and put them all in a glass jar. Put cover on and set them where it is warm so they will rot in good shape, and in the fall add a little fish oil and you will have something that will smell right loud.

Most anything that will smell strong is good scent, but no matter how good your bait and scent is, you must have the trap so the fox can't smell it, and know how and where to set it. Don't forget to set your trap where there are foxes. This is one thing to keep in mind, always set where you see signs. Some think they can set a trap any old way and place, and ought to make a catch, and then get discouraged. If you don't get your game the first night try again and keep right on trying; it is courage and grit that makes a successful trapper. Look for signs whenever you are in the woods, and study them and the animals that you want to catch. I always look up places in summer, and when the time comes to set traps I know just where every trap is going and how many I want.

I tried a great many times to catch a fox before I was successful. I remember one time I got an old horse for fox bait in winter, and put him in a good place. We had a snow storm a few days afterwards, and boylike I started with my rabbit dog and gun to look for rabbits and to take a look at my old horse to see if the foxes had begun to feed on him, and when I got to him he was a sight to behold. The snow was all trodden down solid around him where they had circled and stood around and fed on him. That was too much for me. It took the rabbit fever all out of me for that day, and I started for home to get six No. 2 1/2 Newhouse traps to set around the horse, and I could not get home quick enough to suit me.

I had always wanted to catch a fox so bad and I thought the time had come. I set them as well as I could and covered them up good, as I thought, and went home. It seemed to me that morning would never come. I knew I was going to have a fox, so I was up early and started after it. When I got almost to the bait I saw new tracks going towards the horse and that made my heart beat a little faster, as I was sure I had one, but they had gone as near as three feet and that was as near as they would go. They knew the traps were there as well as I did, and they never went there as long as my traps were set.

CHAPTER V.

TRAPS AND HINTS.

My idea is that manufacturers make traps too strong for the animal it is made for, says C. F. Keith. Now the No. 2 is too strong for fox, and also it is very hard to conceal from view.

Of course if you get a fox in a No. 2 you are more sure than if he is caught in a No. 1 1/2 or smaller. I use the No. 1 1/2 Newhouse for fox and I find it the best fox trap made. I have also used the Jump and the Blake & Lamb, but I do not like them as well. Some trappers think that the Blake & Lamb are the best mink traps made. I beg leave to differ with them, for the simple reason that I have lost many a mink by the trap cutting off the leg and the mink escaping, which never happens with the Newhouse.

The Blake & Lamb trap are, without doubt, the best trap to conceal, but when it comes to be the best trap it is not in it with the Newhouse. I think if trappers would use long chains when using clogs, they would have better luck in trapping the fox. The kind of traps I use are the No. 1 1/2 Newhouse for fox, with four foot chains. When I first began to trap fox I used cheap traps, and many a fox have I lost by not knowing enough to use good traps. By all means, trappers, buy good traps in the first place and you will not be sorry.

Now let me first give you a few pointers on fox trapping. First, forget everything you have bought from humbugs and use common sense; second, study the habits of the fox and you will have better success. Third, be sure and have your traps in proper shape so the fox can't smell the iron; fourth, be careful in making a set, use the wooden paddle or gloved hand in placing dirt over trap; fifth, be sure that your bait is not scented with human scent, and use cat, skunk, or muskrat scents.

I have bought scent for many years, but the best scent I can find is skunk essence or oil of anise. Skunk essence and honey equal parts, but never use skunk essence in early winter, as it will be a failure. I have trapped fox for many years and I am very successful and lucky, and every fall I believe I learn something.

Another thing, never get discouraged, for it is grit that counts. When a fox turns the trap over reset it and place another trap in the bed, and you are liable to catch him the first night, but if this fails, turn trap bottom side up and he will get fooled, sometimes, not always, for fox trapping is uncertain.

In the first place, when an animal gets into a trap he tears around for a while, says G. F. Moon, of Dakota, and if the trap be lightly clogged so he can move around, the trapper most generally finds his game when he visits the traps. On the other hand, let the trap get fastened solid and the animal sets his reasoning powers to work; he finds out that he can chew from the under side of the jaws of the trap, and that too without giving himself any pain, and finds that he can easily slip the trap off from the stump of his leg.

Man has been known to do the same thing, when by accident he has been caught by the leg by a tree or a large rock falling on him. Surely the animal showed as much reason as the man. I once had a large fox trap set in a hollow log. The log was about the size of a barrel. A she fox got into the trap, and as the trap was a good bit out of the way I did not visit it for several days. When I did visit the trap the snow was all tramped down by foxes around the log and on the inside of the log by the fox in the trap. There were the remains of several rabbits and one whole rabbit fresh killed, one fresh killed quail and feathers enough to have been on a couple more quail. Now the question arises, "Did the other foxes let instinct guide them to feed the unfortunate fox in the trap? Or did they use their power of reason?" I leave that for others to answer.

CHAPTER VI.

ALL ROUND LAND SET.

I have made a close study of the red fox for years and the all round land set is one of my best and latest sets, says J. H. Shufelt, of Canada. First used last year and took 15 red foxes, and when properly and carefully set, is the most killing method I ever used.

How to make the scent--This scent should be made in August, of house cat, muskrat or skunk, chopped fine and put in a two quart glass jar and sealed until it forms a liquid, and should fill the jar two-thirds full. Two weeks before using put in the musk of one skunk, one oz. oil of amber, and enough skunk oil to nearly fill the jar; get a new paint brush, a small one will do, and see that it is clean, to use scent with, and it should be kept in the jar.

How to fix trap--I prefer a waxed trap. I find a smoked trap will rust on the under side after setting about a week. It's not so with a waxed trap. If properly waxed, water will not rust them. Take a large kettle of hot water and keep it boiling hot. Melt your beeswax in a cup or dish and pour on the water; now take your traps, six at a time, and dip them, and the wax will adhere to them; just leave the traps in the water long enough to warm them a little, when the wax will spread evenly over them; drain over kettle and hang up to dry a week before using. One half pound of wax is sufficient for three dozen traps and chains and will last one trapping season.

How to set the trap--I use rubber boots and set in the morning when the dew is on the grass or on a wet day. The set should be made near the foxes' runways or on high ground; dig out a place the size of your trap, take something with you to put the trap and dirt on--for this purpose I use a piece of oil cloth, two feet square--fill all around outside of your trap with fine dirt, and put a large leaf over your trap. I use a large leaf from a first growth basswood. As soon as they fall from the tree I gather them and lay them flat together in the mud until I want them to use. Why I prefer this particular kind of leaf is, they grow so large that one leaf covers the trap. After the leaf is over your trap cover with fine dirt or something that must be in keeping with the surroundings. Now stand in one place and take your brush from the jar and paint a circle about two feet in diameter, the width of your brush on the grass all around your trap. This should be repeated once or twice a week, especially after a heavy rain storm. Nothing can steal your bait, John Sneak'um cannot locate your trap.

When visiting your traps carry an extra trap along, and when you make a catch set a clean trap by exchanging traps; always clean your trap after making a catch before setting again. Now boys, start in right, by using a good trap with a large pan, one that can be easily concealed. Don't try to catch a fox with a weak trap, for you will only be disappointed and at the same time be educating another fox, and he will make the rest shy, for they often travel in pairs. When making your sets, don't disturb anything around the place nor use a bush drag where there hasn't been one, for the fox is quick to notice. Use a grapple that can be concealed under your trap. Just try and see how slick a set you can make and try and learn the habits of the animal you are trying to catch, for that is the key to success.

CHAPTER VII.

SNOW SETS.

Much has been said pro and con relative to trapping that most wary of our wild animals, the red fox. A few incidents pertaining thereto that have come under my observation may be worthy of mention, says J. A. Newton, of Michigan.

There are practically three conditions under which trapping the fox may be done. First, by setting in beds, so called, of dry chaff or ashes before snow falls; secondly, in snow during the coldest weather, and lastly spring water setting as some writers have described.

I shall confine myself to the two first mentioned conditions. In the first instance a spread of chaff or ashes covering three or four feet of space is made where foxes are known to travel. As a rule the most acceptable bait is lard scraps, suet, smoked meat rinds, etc. These are scattered in small bits in the bed, and as a lure nothing can be more efficacious than a few drops sprinkled in the bed composed of the female fox gland taken in the rutting season that has been dissolved in alcohol. It must be kept tightly corked. The same taken from the female dog at this period is about as potent.

The traps must first be thoroughly smoked with some resinous twigs or corn cob, or be boiled in ashes to eradicate the scent of iron, rust, and of other game that has been caught. After this do not handle traps or bait except with gloves.

All old trappers in my section bait a fox a few nights before placing the trap, as the more visits Reynard makes to the bed, and devouring bait without having his suspicions aroused, the more reckless does he become and the easier is he taken when at last the trap is placed.

One old trapper, who is very successful, does not set his traps until some night when the first snowfall is at hand. The new white mantle covers the bed and all human sign made in setting the trap. The clog should have been previously placed some days before so that the fox will become accustomed to the sight of it. The fox has not forgotten the exact location of the bed with its tidbits and comes to it with unerring precision even when covered by snow, and unless he by good luck kicks the trap over and springs it he now comes to grief.

Old man Titus says: "Having nailed the game don't kill on the spot but drag him off a ways. Then don't leave the carcass lying round conspicuous or it will scare the rest out of the neighborhood."

My first insight into the manner of snow trapping I gained from a man named Williams. Several of his sheep concluded to part company with this cold unappreciative world, and their owner determined to make them still serve a purpose. Hauling them off in as many directions as there were of the dead, he left them until deep snow and severe weather came, cutting off much of the natural prey of the fox which reduced him to seeking carrion. After their inroads on the bait had become well established, Williams placed a trap at each of the remains, covering a little snow over them and stapling to pieces of fence rails previously placed.

"Now," said Williams, "the only thing to do is to keep away from here two or three days until a little more snow falls to cover our sign, or is drifted a little by the wind." He used no scent of any kind, saying that "starvation is the best lure in the world." "All I do is to smoke the traps and not handle barehanded," he added.

After two or three days of snow flurrying weather we visited the traps and noted that one was missing. We could see a dim trail where it had been dragged away. We followed and found the fox in a drift. He was poor and had frozen hard. Five were taken at the sheep bait inside of two weeks, after which there came a thaw stopping further snow trapping.

One old trapper tells of a fox that came near outwitting him, being not only the most cunning but also possessing a degree of meanness almost satanic. "I baited him in a bed of chaff several nights," said he, "and then set my trap. The trap could not have contained scent, but the old chap appeared to know it was there; he carefully nosed out and devoured every scrap of bait, and then as deftly dug the trap out, turned it over and sprung it and left a soiling evidence of his scorn and contempt for me upon it. That I was mad you needn't doubt for a minute. I tried setting three and four traps, hoping he'd make a miscue and get into some one of them, but no, he was too smart, he sprung them all each night and insulted me besides. All at once the thought struck me like a brick, I'll set the trap bottom side up. This I did, removing all the traps but one. "The cat came back" and as before turned the trap, bringing it right side up. I had set it full catch so that it would spring rather hard. He slipped a cog in not taking into account that the trap didn't spring when he turned it; when bestowing his disdain a too close contact brought a sharp click and he was fast. I never saw so sneaking and beat out an animal in my life. He would like to have had the ground open up and swallow him if it could."

An acquaintance of mine who is a settler in Northern Michigan heard a great squealing and commotion among his hogs one night late in November, and bounced out just in time to see a large bear drop one of his shoats as it passed through the bars. The porker was stone dead, being bitten through the nape of the neck. The settler, whose name is Clark, drew the pig into the woods and left it between two fallen trees. With his axe he chopped a niche large enough to contain a trap, when set, from each of the logs; a piece of moss was carefully fitted over each cavity and all of the chips were removed.

Foxes there are very numerous, and Clark soon noticed that the bait was being sampled; he knew the fox nature in that they have a habit of walking logs or on the highest points when investigating an attraction. When the tracks to and from and circling the bait became frequent Clark placed a trap on each log, covering them neatly with patches of moss; the chain was fastened to clogs concealed under the logs, and the chains were hidden with strips of moss. Upon his first visit to the traps, two days later, the trapper found a fox in each trap, and several more were taken before crows and other scavengers had polished the bones of the bait.

On the quiet, boys, I will say that it requires so much preparation, caution and patience to successfully trap the red fox that I have more frequently resorted to the hound and shotgun; by this means I have often taken the jacket of a cunning old dog fox, after running him over the hills an hour or two, that it would have taken much time and patience to trap. After one gets the runways learned, and if he possesses a good gun that loads properly, and is a tolerably fair shot at running game, the means is much quicker. It is like digging out a nest of skunks as against the slow process of trapping one at a time.

I had a little experience with a sly old female fox last winter, says Claude Roora, of Ohio. I had noticed on early snows where this old fox had two holes under an old rail fence where she would pass through every night, and also a stone beside a sheep path where she would stop. I picked out those three places to set traps for her under the next snow.

One morning I thought it looked as though it was fixing for a snow. I got three No. 2 Victor traps and told my wife I was going to catch that old fox that night if it snowed. I went to the three places and was very careful not to tear things up any more than just to dig places the size of the traps. I had grapnels fastened to chains and dug holes deep enough to bury them, so that when the traps were set on top of them it would be just a little below level of the surface of the ground, and covered all up with dead grapevine leaves. About the time I got the last trap set it commenced snowing and quit snowing before dark.

Next morning I went early to get my fox before the hound men got out, thinking sure I would have her. When I got within one hundred yards of set No. 1 I saw her tracks leading straight to it. She went up within five or six feet of the trap, turned short off to the right and went down to set No. 2, went up within five or six inches of trap where she turned short off to the right again, made a few jumps down the hill, jumped over top of fence, circle back up the hill to sheep path, followed it out to set No. 3. She went up to this trap, raked every bit of snow and leaves off of trap and left trap bare and in plain sight, not even springing trap. I covered trap up again thinking I might fool some other fox, but in about half an hour the hounds came along on her track and one of them set his foot in the trap and his owner let him loose and threw the trap away.

The hounds followed the fox up over the hill, routed it and ran it about an hour and holed it under a big rock, and the men went off and left it. Now the hounds had been in the habit of holing this fox under the same rock, and the most of us know that when a pack of hounds hole a fox they generally tear things up some. In other words, they leave some signs. I set the traps as nice as I knew how, and when I went back the next morning traps were turned upside-down and fox gone.

So I concluded I would follow the track and see if I couldn't find her asleep and shoot her, but had not gone far when I found the snow had drifted so I could not follow her. I came back home discouraged. Next morning I thought I would go and see if she had been back on the hill. When I got to set No. 2 I saw where she had come up from the opposite side from what she had been in the habit of doing and stuck her right foot square in the trap. She went about one hundred yards where she got tangled in some grapevines and was waiting for me.

Now I think there are instances where the scent of steel or human scent will scare animals away from your sets, and when you mix them both together they are a sure warning of danger with all shy animals. Now if this fox did not locate that trap at set No. 3 with her nose I would like to know how she did it, for I removed every bit of dirt I took out to make set and left all level and two and a half inches of snow ought to make things look as natural as any fox could expect to find a set, and at a rock where she had been in the habit of seeing things torn up by the dogs when she came out on previous occasions, and traps hidden out of sight, her nose surely told her where they were set.

CHAPTER VIII.

TRAPPING RED FOX.

In the many years that he has been striving for his glossy pelt, man has evolved numerous clever schemes for outwitting the fox, but in the meantime Reynard has not been an idle observer regarding the ways of the human enemy, says J. L. Woodbury, of Maine. He lacks the advantage of books or tradition for handing down his store of accumulated knowledge, but in some mysterious way it is transmitted from generation to generation, nevertheless. So it is that the fox of the older and more thickly settled sections is a very different animal from the fox--even though it be of the same variety or species--inhabiting a part of the country where its kind has not been so persistently hunted. Tricks that prove effective with the latter are utterly lost on his better-schooled brother. Hence the simple methods advanced by some trappers are a bit amusing to the trappers here in the East, where the subject of this sketch reaches the acme of wisdom, and is, we believe, the peer in shrewdness and cunning of any animal in the world. However, we do not wish to be understood as ridiculing anybody's methods. We read the crudest of them with interest, realizing that they are all right in the region whence they came.

I would advise the amateur fox trapper to begin with the water set if practicable. Nearly any one of the many different forms are good enough, with such modifications as will be found necessary to adapt it to varying conditions of different sets. As one should not begin operations until freezing weather, spring water should be selected for the trap. A good-sized spring works best, but if this is not to be had, utilize some of the little springs to be found in plenty near the sources of brooks. One with a dark bottom is to be preferred, as then there will be no sand to clog the trap, which may be pressed down into the mud until it is all hidden but the pan. This should be about an inch under the water, and covered with a lump of moss.

The position of trap with relation to bait has so often been explained I need not dwell upon it here. If the spring be a large one it is easy to place the bait so that it will be protected by water on all sides save the one desired, but if a smaller pool be employed the side opposite the trap should be barricaded with stumps or brush; which work, by the way, had better be done some time during the previous summer. And rather than leave too narrow an approach to the bait if is better to set two or even more traps, for reynard's suspicions are quickly aroused by anything resembling an inclosure.

As to the matter of bait, it may be said in general that foxes like about all kinds of meat. Yet the task of selecting a killing bait is not always as easy as might be expected from this, as individuals seem to have their particular preferences, while the morsel that would be eagerly sought by the same fox at one season will have no attraction for him at another. If you find "signs" in the vicinity of your sets, yet they remain unmolested, experiment with different kinds of baits, as the angler tries a variety of flies at every likely-looking pool. It is certain that mice, rabbits and grouse are among the best baits.

For the "scent" part, some trappers claim to do well without them, but a good scent is unquestionably a great help. Many of those for which receipts are given I know to be effective. But the most tempting bait and the strongest lure will jointly prove unavailing if one's set be unskillfully made, and carelessness be practiced in going to and from trap.

Water, of course, leaves no scent where it is possible to reach the set by boat or wading, but where this is impracticable arrange to go to trap but rarely, if it remain undisturbed. The height of springs vary but little with wet or dry weather, and this fact should be taken full advantage of by the fox-trapper. Carefully select a trap that will not spring of itself. See that the trigger is pushed well into the notch, pick out a good, close-fibred piece of moss for pan, not large enough to clog the jaws, and stick a few small twigs around it to hold it in place. Push the chain well down into the mud, have the bait exactly in the right place, and in fact use every care to have things fixed so that they will not be disarranged by trivial causes. Then in visiting, go no nearer than is necessary to see that bait or trap have not been disturbed.

Skunks will often prove a great bother, as they take all kinds of bait and kick up no end of a "bobbery" when caught. The fact that their pelts pay the bill in part is but poor consolation, when one has just got a particularly shy old red coat about worked up to the "biting" point.

Sometimes one will run upon natural conditions particularly favorable for a set--a rock, islet or piece of drift in mid-channel, or an old log spanning the stream. Experienced trappers are quick to note all such places as these, as well as points where, with a very little human handiwork, traps may be placed to advantage.

It is best to make all essential preparations as long before setting as possible, though bearing in mind that the streams are usually much higher in the trapping season than during the summer. Also begin putting out baits some time before setting traps. No animal exercises afterward the same degree of caution as on the first two or three visits to a spot, and even so shy a creature as the fox, if he become accustomed to picking up a few choice bits at a place, will soon neglect much of his usual precaution in approaching it, and though he take alarm and shun it for a time will ere long get up sufficient confidence to renew his visits.

If you find where there is a burrow with a family of young foxes, watch them all you can during your leisure moments. Learn where they get their food, where they cross the streams, and their general lines of travel. True, the family may be broken up and driven to sections miles away before time for trapping, but nevertheless a few traps should be placed in the old beats, as if one of this family should ever return to the vicinity he will be certain to revisit his former haunts.

Many trappers, and especially young trappers, expect to get a fox the first night, and, as it would seem, think to make their set so that not the slightest taint of man or iron lingers about the spot after they leave it. They boil their traps in this or that, or smear them with some odorous substance (the very thing perhaps to draw the game's attention to them); they handle them gingerly with gloves (which are often as strongly imbued with man smell as their naked hands); strap hides, pieces of board or snow shoes to their feet when setting or visiting, and in fact go through a rigmarole that would require about half a day to set a single trap. Then they think that if the shyest old fox imaginable should come along that night he would walk into their snare as confidently as a cow into a stall, or a man into his own house. Without reflecting upon the methods of any one, we must say that we consider many of these expedients unnecessary, unless when dealing with an unusually shrewd customer.

For my own part we make but little reckoning on a trap for the first two or three days, especially one with bait. Sometimes, of course, a storm helps us out, or we may nab a youngster who is green at the game; but this is an exception, not the rule. We take all needful precautions in respect to disturbance and scent, but our chief aim is to secrete and cover our trap well; to cover it so that no smell or iron can possibly reach the surface, and so that it will remain covered for weeks if necessary, and yet be ready for business, let the weather be what it will--snow or rain, heat or cold. Herein lies the essence of the art; to fix your trap so that it will not soon require your attention, then nature will speedily dispose of whatever scent you may have left about it. We are speaking now chiefly of land sets.

In looking up a place for a set, select one if possible where some natural or artificial provision will admit of approach without leaving much scent--a hard-beaten path, a double stone wall, a line of ledges, or a combination of some such conditions, which should be invariably followed in going to and from trap.

When you have decided upon the place for a trap, make all possible preparations at a distance; then go to the spot and do your work as quickly and cleanly as you can. If the ground is soft, use a strip of board to stand on. If you use gloves, have some especially for the purpose, and never leave them lying about your dog's quarters or the house. It will do no hurt to smear them lightly with whatever you are using for scent.

See that the trap rests evenly and firmly, so that if any part of it be stepped on it will not tip and pull apart the covering, or grate upon rocks or the chain. Make your excavation quite deep, filling in the bottom with some two inches of hemlock twigs or something of like nature, so as to prevent the gathering of moisture and a consequent freeze. Secure to a clog, or use a grapnel. The latter is in most cases preferable, as it may be buried from sight, while the former adds one more to the objects likely to arouse suspicion.

The covering is something that you will pretty much have to learn for yourself. Like swimming, no one can teach it by any amount of talking; practice is necessary to acquire the trick. Moss, leaves and rotten wood are the principal materials used, though pinches of herbage and dirt may be added to harmonize with set and surroundings. Leaves, however, should be used sparingly, as they change shape with every phase of weather, and thus frequently spoil what would otherwise have remained a good covering. If well rotted they give less trouble in this respect, and offer less resistance to the jaws in closing.

When using bait, if not setting in a bed, find a spot where little building is required to protect it--a hollow log or stump, the entrance to an old burrow, a niche in a ledge or hole under a rock. Sometimes, where a trout-stream flows under a step bluff, a little shelf is found in the face of the bluff (and one can usually be made if it is not already there); and by placing a trap on the shelf and the bait just above it, you have sly Mr. Fox at great disadvantage, as he must leap from the opposite side of the brook to the embankment to reach the bait. A projection in the face of a cliff, several feet from the ground, if it is inaccessible from overhead or either side may be similarly improved.

Always be on the lookout for such places as these, where those sharp eyes and that keen, pointed nose will be kept at a distance from your set until it is too late for them to detect signs of danger.

Old roads offer good possibilities for traps without bait. Unused plain roads, where the grass has sprung up may be practically covered by placing a trap in each wheel-rut and the central path. The space under a set of bars may be partly filled with brush and two or three traps placed side by side in the opening with good chances of success. We say two or three traps, as by so doing a larger opening may be left, which adds greatly to your chances. An attempt to coax this slippery fellow into narrow quarters quickly excites his suspicions.

Cow and sheep paths are much traveled by reynard, especially those leading around and through swamps. These are more easily trapped than roads, a good method being to first go along the path with your decoy scent, applying at intervals to objects close beside the path, and then setting traps, without bait, between the "doctored" points. An old pelt of some sort dragged behind you will serve to kill your own scent, and to keep the intended victim to the path.

As stated, an important element of successful fox trapping is to make as little disturbance, and to leave us little scent us possible, in working around, and going to and from trap. It follows then that one should not only aim so to fix his traps that they will require no actual attention under ordinary conditions of weather, except at considerable intervals, but should invariably locate them with a view to being able to look after them in a way not to arouse wily reynard's suspicions.

Sometimes, when trapping along a creek or other waters where it is not convenient to keep a boat, a rude raft may be constructed from which to make sets, and to be employed in visiting same. It simplifies the work one half to be able to do the whole thing by water, as water leaves neither scent nor trail. But where it is not possible to make use of this helpful agent, care should be taken to select a spot that can be approached over ledgy ground, or by jumping from rock to rock, two short strips of board to be stepped upon alternately, being often useful in bridging over any breaks that may occur in such line of approach.

Where this method cannot be employed, owing to the nature of the ground, it is advisable to vary the route in visiting, as by always following the same line a well defined trail will soon be made, which is certain to excite suspicion in an animal as shy as the fox. When dealing with an unusually shrewd customer, some wear snowshoes or strap hide of some sort on the feet, either of which is not a bad plan, as well as that of dragging a fresh pelt behind one to obliterate one's trail.

As to making beds of chaff, while I have no personal experience with this material, it never impressed me as being the proper thing for the purpose, as it is out of place in the woods or fields. If a man comes upon a pile of chaff any where away from buildings, it instantly occurs to him as being queer that it should be in such a place. Do you not suppose that the wild creatures, whose very existence depends upon their sharpness of observation, are likely to note the unfitness of the thing quicker than we? Of course, if the chaff be deposited in place early in the season, allowing time to discolor and decay, it may help the case, or feathers may be thrown over the bed. But in the latter event wind may at any time remove the covering. For myself, I have always had better luck in making sets for any animal with materials obtained from the immediate surroundings, and having therefore nothing foreign in smell or appearance to offend the creature's nose or eye.

Now a few words as to the fox's regard for iron. Does he feel that it is a thing to be avoided or not? It is my belief, brother trappers, that he does, under certain circumstances, have a strong instinctive fear of metal of any kind. That is to say, when he finds it in places where as a rule it is not to be found. The fact that he will walk for miles on the railroad track, and even upon the rails, is no argument to the contrary, for the reason that he has become accustomed to the iron in such places. A large quantity does not alarm him, but a small piece, half hidden in the dirt, in field or wood where he is not accustomed to see it, awakes his distrust. For the same reason, he will trot deliberately out in the road in front of a passing team, when the mere snapping of a twig beneath the hunter's feet would send him off flying. He has learned that danger rarely comes to him from persons traveling by team; it is of the stealthy step and the swift act of raising a gun that instinct has taught him to stand in fear. And so it is with respect to iron. It is all right in its place, he knows, but he also knows that it is quite out of place--from his standpoint, at least--in proximity to his favorite articles of diet. Why even the stupid muskrat, who will go into people's cellars, and in fact most everywhere else he wants to, and who will walk into any sort of set so long as the trap be covered, will not step into a bare trap. Dozens of times have I had my dog follow the tracks one has made around my trap when it was left bare by falling water, but invariably the rat has left the bait rather than put his foot on the uncovered trap. It is absurd to think the thick-headed muskrat is sharper in any respect than wise Mr. Fox.

CHAPTER IX.

RED AND GREY.

I will give a method for trapping the grey fox, and have to say trap him the same as the red fox, as any method that will take one will do for the other, says L. M. Pickens, of Tennessee. The trapper can easily tell which of these species he is setting for, as the grey fox has more of a round track, while his red brother leaves a much larger and longer imprint.

Each of these animals are great rovers, starting on a forage by sunset, traveling many miles in a night; never holing up for the bitterest freeze that comes.

Look for fox tracks in stock paths, old roads not much used, places under fences, washouts, and in large gullies, as such places are their travels, yet many other unnamed places suited risks for your traps may be found if one is closely looking around.

Carry with you a hardwood stick, ready sharpened, with which to dig the pit for your traps, and dig this lengthwise with the path, (not across it), and deep enough so the trap will be just a little below level of surface; now place the trap in, cover over springs and around outside of jaws with dirt, and lay a piece of paper, flat leaves or a piece of cloth over jaws and pan, then pulverize some of the dirt you dug up, sprinkle over the trap 'till all is covered over good, then lay a dead weed or stick on each side of trap two or three inches away, which completes the set.

When you fasten the trap, do not staple it, but wire the ring or end of chain to a bush you cut, one that the fox can drag a distance, which always leaves the same trap pit or hole in readiness for your trap, which should immediately be smoked, set right back for another fox which is sure to come along, and if you are careful he will he yours, as it all depends upon skillful setting and covering the trap chain.

Have everything look as natural when you make the set as before, and I will guarantee the catch of every fox that comes along.

Use none but the best trap, and a Newhouse No. 2 is recommended, handle it and everything about the set with gloves, learn to respect the cunning of a fox by cultivating a habit of standing in one place, always be careful not to spit, whittle or leave any paper about a trap.

Don't use rusty traps, scour off the rust, and boil for thirty minutes in any green bark that will coat them; willow, walnut, or chestnut are good.

Don't lay your traps around on the ground at your sets; better carry them in a satchel, sack or something strapped around your shoulders.

Don't whittle or spit where you are making a set.

Don't staple your traps, but cut and wire the chains to a green limb, one that the fox can drag a distance, and visit your traps regularly, avoiding any unnecessary company.

The method recommended is only the "path method," and to be used altogether without any bait or scents; as I believe the best results are obtained by just taking a fox unawares, and the whole secret is in choosing the place, then knowing just how to conceal the trap, and have everything as natural as possible when the set is made.

Look for fox tracks in stock paths, in pastures, fields, and woods, in large gullies, washouts and places under fences, old roads not much used, sand bars along streams, and other places; always selecting a narrow place for your set; approaching such places with trap ready set and wired to the brush, then with ready sharpened hard wood stick, stop and stand in one place until trap is properly set, when you can just walk right on to the next place.

Always dig the pit just the size of trap to be used, having the springs lengthwise in the path or trail-- not across it--and just deep enough so the trap will be a little below the surface level when put in the pit. Cover over springs and around the outside of the jaws with dirt, lay a piece of paper over pan and jaws, or put fine moss, cotton, wool or dead grass inside of jaws and under pan; then haul on the fine dirt, just enough of it to thinly cover all, brush with a twig to level and complete the set by laying a couple of dead weeds, or small sticks, just haphazard like some two or three inches on each side of the trap.

As soon as you kill your fox, reset the trap in the same pit, but if your brush drag is chewed up, replace it with a new one. In addition, if it is a female fox that is caught, kill it near a path or any good place where a set can be made and where you have lately noticed a fox's track; then conceal and secure your trap as before, and the chances are as good for you to catch one or more fox at this set.

Now try this method all the way through and you will soon see that I am right. My brother set his first fox trap Dec. 9th and on the morning of the 10th had a large female red fox and killed it in a pasture near a path, and that night caught the largest dog fox I ever saw or heard of.

He got both these foxes just exactly as the above method indicates. The dog fox weighed 19 pounds and its hide measured 5 ft. 5 inches on the board. The old fox had lots of gray hairs on his head, evidently an old timer.

CHAPTER X.

WIRE AND TWINE SNARE.

Various are the ways being studied for the capture of the fox and other shy animals, says J. H. Shufelt, of Canada. Most every trapper has a particular method of his own. Years ago trappers thought it was necessary to set in water in order to be successful in catching foxes, but after a closer acquaintance with the ways of the fox, it was found that they were easily caught in a steel trap on dry land in many ways. At the present time the trapper has found a less expensive way of catching them with the snare. This method has many advantages, and when properly set is a sure thing. It takes in most of those old sly ones that have been nipped by steel traps, etc.

The method shown here is only one of the many ways of the snare. Owing to the peculiar fastening of the snare, a powerful spring pole or weight can be used with a lighter wire. I use a copper or brass wire 1 gauge, with a foot or more slack between fastenings, which gives the spring pole a chance to instantly take advantage of the fox as soon as caught, when he will be caught up to the staple (which should be high enough from the ground so the fox will swing clear) and choked.

I set my snares in paths where weeds or grass grow each side to hide the snare. The loop should be seven inches in diameter, ten inches from the ground. It is as well before trapping to get the fox to traveling a path by leaving some good scent along the path. This can be done by boring a three-fourths hole downward in a tree near the path and pour the scent in, which will last a long time. If the same care is used in setting snares as is used in trapping, I think the snare will catch more. They work well in cold weather, and some fine catches can be made after a snowfall with the snare. Then the fur will be good and prime.

A--Spring pole.

B--Staple.

C--Two small nails driven in tree. (Three inch nail head, end down, with snare looped at each end with a foot of slack between. As soon as the D--three inch nail is pulled down, it will slip past the nail at top end, when spring pole will instantly take up the slack, also the fox, to staple and does its work.)

E--Slack line or wire.

F--Loop should be 7 inches in diameter and bottom of loop ten inches from the ground.

Remarks--The nails should be driven above staple so it will pull straight down to release the snare fastening.

I may state that I learned all the best ways of setting traps for fox long ago from an old trapper, says A. H. Sutherland, of Nova Scotia. But I never bothered setting a trap for a fox in my life, for the reason that I can catch them with snares on bare ground much easier and cheaper than with traps. But on snow if I could get fox to take bait, I would try poison on him. I may add that the snare is good for other animals besides the fox, such as coon, skunk and wild cat.

Go to a hardware store and get some rabbit wire and put about five strands of it together, and twist it just enough so that it will stay together nicely. Have a small loop on both ends and run one end through the other so as to make a noose of it. Next get some good twine, put a piece about 10 or 12 inches in length into the loop on the end of the snare, that is, the end that is going to be fastened.

Now find a path in an old clearing or in the woods, and select a place where you think best to set your snare. Cut a stake about 2 feet long and 1 1/2 inches through, have a limb on the butt end of it almost 3/4 inch in length. Sharpen the small end of the stake and drive it in the ground, leaving about 10 or 12 inches above ground; then cut a nice little pole about an inch and a half at the butt end and sharpen it, trim off at about an inch at the top end and fasten your snare, or at least take your pole in both hands and force the butt end into the ground till it will be good and firm.

Now bend down your pole and fasten your snare to it, and put the end of the pole under the catch on the stake. Be sure to drive your stake close enough to the path so as to have your snare light about the center of the path and the lower side of the snare about 8 inches from the ground. It is best to have them high enough so the fox cannot jump over them. Of course a man must use good judgment at setting snares just the same as he would in setting traps.

Another good place is a brush fence. Find holes under it where the fox will be going through, put your snare there, and if there are any going you will have some of them. Next find a good stream in the woods or anywhere frequented by foxes, and if you find good trees that fall across the stream have a good sharp axe and give a good slash or two of the axe about the middle of the tree, or at least above the middle of the brook. As I was going to say, give a good slash or two of the axe lengthwise of the tree and make a wedge shape stake and drive it into the tree, and then fasten your snare to a spring pole. If you prefer, you could bore an auger hole in the log and drive your pin in that way, and fasten the snare to the pin about 10 or 12 inches from the log so that the snare will hang downwards, it will do better. Be sure and have the lower side of snare 7 or 8 inches from the log.

Now there is another kind of brass or copper wire that one strand will be enough to hold a fox. If you find that they are cutting your snares put little rollers of wood in the snare boring a hole lengthwise with a 3/8 bit, and have the roller almost 5 inches long and say an inch in diameter. Put that on snare so it will run down to the side of his neck, and he will keep biting at it.

I get No. 14 brass wire (mind, you must temper the wire) that I find the hardest part of the game. Cut your wire about 34 or 36 inches long, make it into rings round, put in a good hot fire for three or four minutes, or until red. Be very careful and not let it lie on coal, handle very carefully; don't strike against anything while hot, as it will break like glass, but if you have it tempered you cannot break it. I have caught three foxes in the same snare, says Larry Burns, of Canada.

You must make your snare just the same as a rabbit snare, only make a loop about six inches around. Find when the fox passes under a fence or on a cow path, in winter, find where they make a habit of going. Set your snare in such places or around old carrion in bushes, cedar is best, use weeds rolled round your snare, don't use too many as they will notice. Use a green stick to hold your snare fast, You wire about a foot from large end. Always stand up the stick just the same as growing. The stick should be 1 1/2 inches thick. Be careful and make as few foot marks as possible and stand on one side of your snare. While setting don't spit tobacco juice near snare.

A great many foxes have been caught in this country by the plan of the drawing outlined, writes J. C. Hunter, of Canada. A--the snare, should be made of rabbit wire, four or five strands twisted together. Should be long enough to make a loop about seven inches in diameter when set. Bottom side of snare should be about six inches from the ground. E--is a little stick, sharp at one end and split at the other, to stick in the ground and slip bottom of snare in split end, to hold snare steady.

B--is catch to hold down spring pole. C--is stake. D--is spring pole. Some bend down a sapling for a spring pole, but we think the best way is to cut and trim up a small pole about ten feet long; fasten the big end under a root and bend it down over a crotch, stake or small tree. Snare should be set on a summer sheep path, where it goes through the bushes.

Stake might be driven down a foot or more back from the path, where a branch of an evergreen bush would hang over it so as to hide it and a string long enough from stake or trigger to snare to allow snare to rest over path.

Of course, in making this set you will have to use care and your own ingenuity to a great extent, to suit the requirements of the surroundings. Another way is to find a log, tree or pole that lies across a brook that is too wide for a fox to jump from one bank to the other. Set snare on log, but in this case, bottom side of snare should be only about four inches from log, as a fox will carry his nose lower while crossing a stream on a log. If the log is near the water, a spring pole should be used; if the log is high up from the water, fasten snare to log by driving in a wooden pin in the side of the log, and when the fox gets in snare he will tear around, fall off of log and hang all right.

The following is said to be the manner in which they snare foxes in New Brunswick: Early in the season they go into the woods in some favorable locality and build a fence. This place is similar to what would be constructed for partridge snaring, only of course with layer brush, leaving a narrow opening sufficiently wide for the passage of a fox, fixing everything just as they wish it to be later on when ready for business, and having a spring pole at such a distance that it can be utilized when wanted.

Take a dead hen or some kind of meat, place it in a jar, so that it gets well tainted; that when the right time comes place the noose in place at the opening made in the fence, fasten to the spring pole, sprinkle a little of this tainted bait about, and await results.

In going and coming, wooden shoes or clogs are worn, so that the fox will not get the scent of the party setting the trap.

An animal in coming down the path passes its body or neck through the loop made of stout insulated wire; in passing it steps on the trip stick which settles with the animal's weight, releasing the trigger, which in turn releases the stay-wire and jerks the loop around the animal; the spring pole onto which the stay-wire is attached lifts your game up into the air, choking it to death and placing it out of reach of other animals that would otherwise destroy your fur. A small notch cut in the stay crotch where the end of the trip stick rests will insure the trigger to be released. This will hold the trip stick firm at the end, making it move only at the end where the animal stops.

New and valuable methods are continually being published in the Hunter-Trader-Trapper, an illustrated monthly magazine, of Columbus, Ohio.

CHAPTER XI.

TRAP, SNARE, SHOOTING AND POISON.

Some say that scent is no good, and that they can trap more without it, and they even go so far as to offer to match their craft with those using it. I don't call myself a trapper, says E. R. Lafleche, of Canada, as I never spend much time at hunting or trapping. When I go in the woods it is only for a little recreation, and not being an old hunter, I do not know it all yet, but will say that I can get more than my share of foxes in any place here in Canada.

For the benefit of the young as well as many old trappers I will give here my methods of trapping, snaring, shooting and poisoning the fox, which is as good, if not better, than any I have seen. I can clean the foxes out of any section of the country without having to purchase any of the so-called famous scent.

To take away the human scent from whatever I do, I make a bath as follows: First, take 2 lbs. of male cedar branches, 2 lbs. balsam branches, and 1 lb. good hen manure; chop the branches fine and place the whole in a pot in 2 gallons of soft water, "fresh rain water is the best" and boil until reduced to 1 1/2 gallon. Second, take a clean pail or tub, smoke it with birch or balsam bark, then place solution, cover and keep in a temperate place. To make the scent, take equal parts of the following: Fresh eel, honey in comb, chicken, pig liver, mice; chop the whole together like mince meat and bottle, cork and place the bottle in a pail or tub of water so that it will float and in a warm place. A good way is to place the bottle in some shallow part of a lake, creek or river much exposed to the sun, and where the water is warm; use a strong bottle and fill about three-fourths of it, and remove the cork from time to time for fear the fermentation smashes the bottle, and as soon as it has settled, cork well and keep in a temperate place for a week or so, and it is ready for use.

Smear your snowshoes and go where you like, and there will not be a single fox that will come to your trail that will not follow it to the end.

To take the iron smell from traps, first clean them well in warm water. Second, put them in the bath for 10 or 12 hours. Third, smoke them with birch and balsam bark; then they are ready to set, Place the trap 18 inches from the bait and put a few drops of the medicine under the pan of the trap, get a small shovel made of sieve wire, and sieve some snow over the trap and over your signs up to three feet or more from your bait. Don't spit or monkey with pipe and tobacco. Place your bait near a large stone, stump, fence or tree, and in such a way that the fox will be able to approach the bait from side where the trap is; always set the trap so that the loose jaw will be at the far end from the bait.

It is a good thing to place some clean white cotton wool under the pan with a few drops of the scent. As soon as a fox is caught save a front leg and with it print some signs such as a live fox would do, all over the place where the trap is set; also save the urine from the bladder of the fox and when it becomes rancid, sprinkle a few drops on the weeds near the trap and the first fox that will come will be yours.

To poison them strychnine is required. First, use fresh beef suet and make pills the size of a big pea. Second, put the size of a large grain of wheat of strychnine and stick these pills in your bait the same way as garlic in a roast. Third, take a fresh cow head, stick your pills in the fleshy parts of the head, but do not place them too close to each other, then hang the head out of the reach of the hens, etc., in a stable where there is cattle for one night, then take it to the place you wish to leave it and there throw away like a lost head. A good way to place such bait is on a good sized lake. Place the head in the center of it and you will find your fox every time.

Of course when you are using poison you must visit your bait every morning at daylight, so that the drifting snow, etc., will not cover the fox's tracks. While visiting the bait, keep to one side and from three to five feet from it; don't monkey around it, and if Mr. Fox came to the bait and if you have reason to think he has taken a pill, make a circuit of a 100 yards or more until you come to the trail of a fox going away from the bait. As soon as a fox feels the effect of the poison he will make several long jumps and then start to walk.

Follow his tracks, and the moment you notice zigzags in the tracks, or that the fox is looking for an easy place to go through a fence, etc., this is a sure sign that the fox is sick, and you can follow that track and find the fox. Sometimes you will find them not 50 yards from the bait, and other times a half or three-quarters of a mile from the bait. This depends upon the time spent at the bait and is also due to other causes.

A good way to poison them is to place a pill in a mouse or a small piece of liver, but I prefer to make pills with lard, about a square inch, and I insert the poison in the middle of the bullet. To do this, I bore a small hole with a stick, and then place the strychnine and cover the hole with the lard taken from it. To do this with ease, the lard must be partly frozen, smear with honey and keep frozen; then take some frozen liver (any kind will do) and chop it in fine pieces and mix with honey and keep in a small wood box. Smoke the box the same as the traps and smear inside with honey and add a few drops of the medicine. The kind of box I recommend is one 4"x12" made of either cedar or bass wood 1/4 inch thick, with two compartments, one 4"x8" for the liver pieces and the other 4"x4" for the bullets, with a sliding door at each end, and a piece of leather held by small screws on the top for the hand.

When ready, take your ammunition and once on fox land, smear your snow shoes with the scent and at every hundred yards drop a few bits of liver, and at every 500 yards or so, a few more with a pill, and in the pill stick a four inch black feather, and two feet to the right stick a strong weed, and in such a way that the wind will not throw it down. This will enable you to find the pill in case of a snow storm, and by brushing the snow lightly with your mit, the pill can be found at once, unless a fox took it. If the bullet has not been touched you can tell without having to remove the snow, as the feather will stand straight up, and this is a sure sign that the poison is still there. If no feather can be seen and if it has been stormy, brush the snow away, the lard is not as white as the snow and is easily found. Should it be gone, look carefully around the place; sometimes you will see the feather 10 or 20 feet from the place you have placed the pill, and there or elsewhere you should see a place where the fox has been digging a hole. Examine the hole carefully and you may find the poison, as often when not hungry he will hide it for some other time, or for his friend. If you have reason to believe that a fox took the pill, and owing to stormy weather you cannot find him, you must survey the grounds as soon as the snow commences to melt, and by looking carefully along the fences you will often find them. Always keep trace of your pills; the best places to put these is in the middle of a lake or field; the black feather will attract the attention of the foxes at once, and they will make immediately for any black spots they see in a field or on a lake.

To shoot them in winter: Get a complete suit made of white cotton, including cap, smear your suit with scent, or have some balls of cotton wool smeared with it and tie these around your belt with a good string in such a way that you can remove them at will. In a fine moonlight, take your snow shoes and go where the foxes are traveling, and the moment you see one or hear one bark, circle around him so that the wind will carry the scent. He will come towards you and will stop at a certain distance from you, and as you notice him on the alert, stop moving. The fox will put his head up and will look in all directions in order to locate where the nest of the plump mice are, and as you notice this sound the squeal of the field mouse; the fox will at once run toward you; then shoot him. I use BB shot for foxes.

Where foxes are plentiful, a hunter of some experience can bag several in three or four hours. I have killed as many as four in three hours. A good wind, fine moonlight, and lots of foxes, a fellow will have fine sport. In shooting foxes, keep as much as possible on the small hills so as to survey more land. While I was living in the country I had good sport shooting them in the spring, in the high snow banks along the fences.

Foxes are fond of playing at such places, especially when there is a crust to carry them. This generally comes in Canada at the latter end of February and during the month of March. I have often killed them at bait. Horse meat is fine bait for them. I once killed two big foxes at one shot. A hunter can always approach a fox when he is feeding, providing he knows how.

When I trap fox I do it on a large scale. I always set a combination of traps and snares. I carry a good supply of wire snares. The twine must be of dark color. In making a trail for fox, I take advantage of every good place I find either for trap or snares, either between bunches of weeds, trees, stones, stumps, roots, logs, fences, etc., where Mr. Fox will have to pass to follow my trail. On the rail or other board fences I use the twine snare, and on a barbed wire fence, the wire snare. In setting a twine snare, I always use a drop log or stone, and so fixed that as soon as the fox pulls the weight drops, and he is lifted and hung at once. I use ordinary wire fence staples and two to each set, one placed so that when the weight falls the neck of the fox is carried close to the staple and held there, and the other staple close to the drop. The drop must be placed so that it cannot reach the ground, and must weigh about three times as much as any fox.

Any fox that puts his head in the loop is sure to stay there. In the bush, I take advantage of all shanty roads, and I use spring poles when I find a suitable tree. I just trim the head and use a wire snare so that the squirrels, etc., will not bother it.

I set traps at the baits and in the middle of the fields in the same way as poison, with bits of liver around it, and I cover the trap with a light coat of snow with the same little shovel, and under the pan I place some cotton wool with a few drops of scent, and should, while the fox is picking up the pieces of liver, not step on the trap, he is sure to scratch for the mouse under the pan, and the trap will mouse him.

CHAPTER XII.

MY FIRST FOX.

I presume that almost every boy trapper in North America has an ardent wish to trap one of these cunning sharp witted animals, and I remember I thought when a boy if I could only catch a fox in a trap my reputation as a trapper would be made, says F. W. Howard, of Wisconsin.

Boys, you must not be discouraged if, after following the methods you hear, you fail to take a fox, for probably most of you have only traps enough to make one set; any of us older trappers I think will admit that it is rather a difficult feat to make one set and take a fox in a reasonably short time. Most of the trappers who use these sets have likely from a dozen to fifty traps out for fox at one time.

I have sometimes taken foxes in traps set for skunk, coon and mink, so that one may say that with a large number of traps out, even though not set with the care and precautions usually taken to catch a fox, the large number of chances open enable one to take here and there a blundering and unwary fellow. I trapped my first fox when about twelve years old, by following a method given me by my grandfather, who was, in his day, a famous New England fox hunter. He was a very old man at that time, but when I expressed to him my heart's desire, asking him how and where to set the trap (I had but one suitable for fox) he told me to get my father to let me take the oxen and plow, to make a couple of furrows in our back pasture. Following his instructions I boiled the trap in weak lye and then daubed it over with fresh cow manure. The back pasture spoken of was a place where foxes traveled, and I presume that there was no week in the year that at least two or three foxes did not cross there.

Now, this is a very important point, if you are making but one set especially, be sure and find a location for the set near some den or ledge where foxes live, or at some point where you know they are in the habit of crossing. But to continue, under my aged instructor's direction I plowed two furrows across the pasture in the form of an X. "Now," said he, "any fox that comes along will get down and run in the furrows. Set your traps where they cross, and I shouldn't wonder if you found one up here some fine morning." I scooped out a shallow hole of a size to hold the trap and clog, put a bunch of wool under the pan so it would spring easily, and covered all slightly and smoothly with dirt; Granddad then placed some lumps of dirt in such a way that a fox would be apt to step over them into the trap, if coming from any direction. He cautioned me in visiting the trap to walk by it some distance away.

"How long do you think it will be before we catch a fox?", I asked. "Maybe not for a week, and maybe not at all, but I tell you boy, if you want to catch a fox you have got to stick to it." You can imagine my delight the next morning on finding a fine red fox tangled up among some huckleberry bushes near by, and you may be sure I thought Granddad the greatest trapper in the world, and myself the next.

I caught two more foxes at the same set before snow came, and will say that I have always found this method one of the surest, but of course very few boys are situated so as to have pastures that foxes cross, and which they can plow furrows in.

Foxes are generally suspicious of a dead bait;

however, at a bait which they have been in the habit of visiting, generally some carcass, they are more easily caught than at a freshly placed bait or carcass, and it is a good plan, if you try taking a fox in this way, to put out the carcass or large baits long enough in advance for them to get into the practice of coming to them; then place your traps, if possible, just before a fall of snow, and you are almost certain of catching one. The traps should always be set with care and treated as already described, to cover the scent of iron, as a fox considers the scent of man and iron a dangerous combination, and they undoubtedly know about traps and fear them.

I like to use a live bait for fox and bobcats, and a rabbit is about the best for this purpose, because they are easily secured. They form the principal game of these animals and they are nearly always looking for them. It is, I think, safe to say, that each grown fox or bobcat kill two hundred each on an average every year. The sight or hot scent of any game these animals are accustomed to hunt excites them, and their faculties are at once concentrated on how to capture and get on the outside of said game as soon as possible. Under such conditions, they fall more easy prey to trappers' wiles. Select a point where you know foxes hunt, or not far from some den or ledge which they use. Find a hollow log or some tree that has a hollow butt with an opening; in either case, plug the hollow securely so the rabbit will have to stay up near the opening, put in some carrots, or ears of corn, and cover the hole with woven wire, having about an inch mesh, or some barb wire stapled across will sometimes answer;

they may in some cases be afraid of the wire, but I have had excellent success with this method, and my opinion is that the sight of live game makes them reckless (on one occasion I caught a fox in a wooden box about eight inches square and three or four feet long, having a wire door, hinged at the top and slanting in,--a self-setter--the trap had a live rabbit inside and was set along a creek, for the purpose of taking a mink alive and uninjured).

If this method is used as a snow set, brush out all tracks, and whether on snow or bare ground, always make as few tracks and leave as little sign as possible around your traps. When setting for any shy animal, don't cover or handle trap or clog with bare hands. Use gloves and a small wooden spade.

CHAPTER XIII.

TENNESSEE TRAPPER'S METHODS.

Do you trap foxes? If you do I bet you have some favorite way, and too, doubtless in most respects it's different from my way of trapping them, as there seems to be almost as many methods as there are successful trappers; nor either is the same confined to the methods used, but to the kind of traps employed, baits, scents, etc., says B. P. Pickens.

The Water Set, the Sheep Path Methods, are national, and known to be O. K., though the former requires bait attractions, and lots of other preparations, while the latter with me has never necessarily required baits or scents to make it a good success.

I do not confine my fox trapping to any one method long, for I am always governed by the surroundings, and conditions, yet my traps are set and concealed the same way, no matter for what animals I intend to trap.

My traps set for skunk and rats are just as carefully set and concealed as though they were set for fox and coon.

My favorite is a Newhouse Fox Trap for every purpose, as it will hold.

My reasons for using nothing smaller than a No. 2 Fox Trap is that a fellow does not always know if a fox will happen about his skunk traps or a big coon about his rat traps, and since I have found Mr. Fox and Mr. Coon a few times in the toils I make every preparation for his reception.

I will endeavor to tell some of the things I do, which is a good way to take a fox. I commence early in the spring, if the ground is not ready to arrange for my fall and winter trapping, looking out for their signs, and continue to keep my eyes open all summer and around the pastures, in the fields, old roads, and in the woods, gullies and washouts. I arrange to trap them in stock paths by laying a limb or fence rail across these paths, while the use of stock all summer renders it old, and on either side of this path obstruction is just the place for a fox trap. I cut and wire my trap chain to the middle of a brush, one that a fox can drag some distance away, which leaves this same place a good risk for another catch, where if stapled to something he could not move he would render the place unfit for the rest of the season.

Conceal your trap by digging a hole on either side of the path obstruction the size of the trap to be used, setting trap always springs with path, have the hole deep enough so when the trap is well covered with leaves, then on the leaves a layer of dirt, it will just be level with the earth and look natural.

To use this same underground method in cold freezing weather, first bed the trap hole good with dry leaves, or grass, over springs and all, being sure to use dry flat leaves to lay over the pan and jaws, then cover over all with some of the remaining dirt before mentioned.

Be sure to hide chain and handle everything with gloves.

Now brush out your tracks, step over your trap and go on.

One way of trapping foxes may be done like this. Around the pastures and in the woods where stock make paths lay a fence rail, or its equivalent across these paths, and the use of stock during the summer months will render these prearranged obstructions worn and natural by November trapping, and on either side of such an obstruction is a splendid place to set your trap for the fox to step in, writes L. M.

Pickens.

Paths, places under fences, little washouts, and old roads not much used are generally his favorite travels. See after his tracks in the dust, mud, or snow; notice how he steps over one of these obstructions that you arranged early in the summer, and other places, studying him, then set your trap this way, using every precaution to not change any of the surroundings.

Carry with you a little hard wood stick, ready sharpened, with which to dig a hole on either side of this obstruction that has been lying over the stock path just the size of your trap, and deep enough so your trap pan and jaws will be a little below the level of the surface. Now cover over springs good and all around the outside of jaws with some of this dirt you dug up; now you have the trap concealed all but its pan and inside of jaws; finish the set by laying some small flat leaves from jaws to pan, commencing and going all the way around jaws; after this is done pulverize some of the remaining dirt, and sprinkle it over these leaves, entirely covering them. Take a small twig and level over trap, finishing the job. It might help some to cut a part of a bird into fine pieces, dropping it and loose feathers over this kind of a set.

To fasten the trap is some of the job. Cut a bush with a lot of limbs to it, and wire your trap to the middle of same securely, but do not have the brush drag so heavily that he cannot run off with it; it is intended for him to go immediately after he is caught, for these reasons, he will soon hang up some distance away, and thus fastened, he is not stationed at this good place where another may be caught, besides his chances of pulling out of the trap is less than it is if he was stapled to something he could not move. The brush is a give and take game, see?

Be sure to cover chain of trap good, and have everything look as natural when you leave us when you came to set trap. Use No. 2 Newhouse, handling it and everything with gloves; always stand In one place; leave no paper or whittlings on the premises. I use this method just outlined. Try it boys.

CHAPTER XIV.

MANY GOOD METHODS.

There is no animal roaming the woods so hard to catch in a steel trap as the fox, says a writer in the *Orange Judd Farmer*. Yet when one understands his nature he is easily taken despite his cunning. The following method I have employed successfully: First take four good steel traps and cover them with fresh blood at a slaughter house. Take a dead hen (one that has died a natural death will do if there is no odor), and run a wire up in her head and down in her body; also wires through her feet and legs. Select a place where foxes run near a low bush or small tree. On a branch of this, about three feet from the ground, fasten your hen solidly with the wires in her feet. By means of wire in her neck, bend it so she will look as if she were on a roost. Be very particular on this point. Set your trap a little below the surface of the soil, so that the tops are level. Now cover up with leaves and grass so that there is no difference in appearance from the surrounding ground. Be sure the chains are well staked. Mr. Fox comes up and sees the hen. He squats down on his stomach. He will lie there for five minutes watching the hen. Then he makes a spring for her neck, and gets it, but the traps get him and the boy gets the fox if he is cute enough.

Well here is how I caught my first fox, says C. F. Hotchkiss, of Wisconsin. It was in the winter of 1887 and 1888. I was working for a farmer here in Shawano Co., had to drive the stock to the river to water all winter. I noticed fox tracks on the ice so I bought a double spring Newhouse. Gave 60 cents for it, took some chaff from the hay in the cow stable for a bed and set the trap on the river bank under a large hemlock to protect it from storms, covered trap with chaff and strewed pieces of chicken and feathers on the bed. In four days I had two foxes, then some one stole my trap and I did not try any more then. Last winter I was working for the same farmer again. He lost two sheep. We drew the carcasses out in the woods, set four traps at one sheep and six at the other. In seven weeks we had 14 foxes and we lost no time from other work. We pulled wool from the sheep to cover the traps with. I do not think it best to spit near a fox trap, especially tobacco spit. There may be some foxes that do not care for it, but I know they are not all built that way.

One of my methods of trapping Reynard was as follows: First, thoroughly besmear the trap with droppings from cattle, using no other preparation, neither boiling or smoking, as some recommend to prevent their fear of human scent, then my favorite sets being in the path of some old timber or wood road or cattle path in some unusual pasture. After selecting the place best suited, according to my best judgment, take a knife to cut out a hole corresponding to size of trap, remove carefully all loose earth. I usually carried a small basket for the reception of everything taken up this way. Set the trap carefully, covering loosely with some coarse material and topping the whole with material to correspond with the surrounding surface of paths, and lastly laying a small twig across just at one side of where the trap is set, as a fox will always step over any small obstruction, and by placing the twig in this manner he would step over into the trap.

In the section of country which I am now writing, that just east of the White Mountains in New Hampshire, there were innumerable such roads and paths, so that I had all the territory I desired for the purpose. Have caught many a sly chap in this manner. Had a good grapple at end of chain and never fastened a trap but let them make a few jumps when they would nearly always get caught up, yet on a few occasions have had to put up a pretty stiff hunt before locating them. For instance, there might be a snow storm, if late in the season, or a heavy rain. In this case there might not be any signs to go by, and I would have to go on a blind hunt and cover considerable ground before I could skin my fox.

I had my traps all set one fall and everything was coming my way, until one morning I found that I was dealing with a fox that knew as much about trapping as I did. I had my trap set in a spring and every time he wanted to steal bait he could manage it without getting into the trap. I let the trap set the same way and kept it baited but meanwhile I was thinking of a plan to capture him. In fixing the spring I made a dam out of dirt, placing a few small flat stones on top of it. Now I made up my mind that as the dam was the nearest point to the bait that he must be stealing it from that place. Now I took the trap out of the spring and put in a stone covered with a tuft of grass to resemble the trap and setting the trap itself in the dam, covering with dirt and laying a little flat stone on the pan. I had made up my mind that when he stepped on the dam he would step on the small stones that I had laid on top to keep the dirt from washing away. While stepping on the dam to reach for the bait he stepped on the small stone on the pan and was held fast by a No. 2 1/2 Blake & Lamb trap, just as I had calculated on.

One way of trapping fox is setting under water, especially in slow moving water, is most effectual in killing the trap odor, says a Michigan trapper. The metallic smell will not rise through water, but will be absorbed and carried away by it. As much as a fortnight before setting take a hoe and dig a shallow pool in a swamp where foxes are known to cross. Dig it six or seven feet across in a mucky ooze and leave a drain way or outlet open so that in event of rain storms, water will not rise and stand too deep in the pool. The pool should bear as few evidences as possible of having been made by man.

In the course of a fortnight after the scent of the trapper has faded away and leaves have fallen, the trap is smeared with tallow and the chain is fastened to long narrow stone, approaching so as to make and leave as few tracks as possible. The trap along with the stone and chain is set in the bottom of the pool, not in the center, but so near one side that the trap will be from 12 to 14 inches from the low bank. A little tuft of grass as large as a soda biscuit is placed directly over the trap resting on it, so the top of the tuft will show a little above the water, looking as though it grew there. About a foot beyond it further out in the water another tuft a little larger and thicker, is placed so it will show distinctly above the water, and on it place the bait. A fox crossing the swamp on a chilly day scenting the bait will approach the pool. To avoid wading in the cold muddy water he will probably step on the nearest tuft. That is the one on the trap in which he will be caught by the foreleg.

I will tell you what I know about the fox, says a Canadian trapper. He is the slyest animal we have to deal with here. I think the best way is to use several different ways to trap foxes, and your chances will be doubled in taking them.

Take a horse or beef head and put it out in the woods and leave it there for about a week. Then if the foxes have been at it, set your traps and cover with leaves or dead pine needles. When you are leaving take a brush and brush some snow over your traps to about half cover the leaves. Leave no foot marks around and you will be pretty sure to get your fox.

Another good way is to take tainted beef or pig kidneys and put them at the back of a V, made by two logs falling across each other. I took one this way before the snow came, but he got away with my trap.

I have read and heard a lot about human scent and animals being afraid of it. I have seen enough to be sure that fox are not afraid of either human scent or steel traps, if the dirt is not disturbed around the trap.

When snow is plentiful so that sly Reynard may be tracked, then search out his haunts and find where he sleeps in the day time, says a Canadian hunter. They seldom go in holes in the winter, and in the bright sunny days are very sleepy. In tracking you will see marks where they have been lying, generally in some elevated position close to their haunts, where they may be caught napping as they often are caught. The snow should be soft so as to make the least noise possible, but it is astonishing the amount of noise you can make and still not disturb them, providing you have been thoughtful enough to keep the wind in your favor, as they are very quick to smell a person, so in consequence you should always face the wind and go easy in your search. The snow shoes are a great help when the snow is deep, as it is then that the fox is easiest gotten as they will not go far in the deep snow. Try it boys and be surprised at your success.

I will try and explain to you my method of catching fox alive, writes Howard Hurst, of Pennsylvania. Take a common box trap, put a wire partition about

4 inches from back end of trap. On the back end of trap put a wire door that you can open and shut. Take the trap to some good den, take a small live chicken and put in the back part of trap. The noise of the chicken will attract the foxes' attention and he will enter the trap door. I saw four caught this way last spring by a boy 9 years old.

I will mention how you can get a fox without bait, says Jarvis Green, of Maine. Look up an old path or wood road where you see that they have traveled, and notice a mound or rise of ground; now the foxes always stop to urinate on all such places. When you see the wind and atmosphere indicates a fall of snow, go and set your trap, smear with balsam of fir, cedar, hemlock or spruce, set your trap on center of mound and on one side stick up a tree branch to look as if grown there, about eight inches high, fasten trap to a clog by the middle, cover trap lightly with some fine substance. A drop or two of scent is sure of every one that comes along. Try this. The Blake & Lamb trap is best. I have only one fault with the single spring and that is the trencher is too large. On the new style if the animal steps on the edge of trencher, result is a toe or two will be left. Be careful in covering trap so that when it springs the jaws will shut tight.

When I was a boy I used to hunt foxes with dog and gun. In tracking them I noticed that they would go to every skunk that was killed, writes L. M. Cartwright, of Pennsylvania, near where they traveled, and nose around, but never saw where they ate any of it, so I used the scent successfully in catching them. I have caught many of them in No. 1

Newhouse trap fastened to a clog; had one to pull the staple out of a clog and carry trap as much as five miles before catching him, and if it had not been for a fresh fall of snow would have been out.

About as sure a way to catch fox (if you have the proper place) is to snare him. Here they very often cross the creek on logs or trees that have fallen across, when the creek is not frozen over. Take about three and a half feet of wire, such as is used for baling hay, make a snare, staple or spike the end of wire down on the side of the tree about the center of the creek, bend wire up so the loop comes over the center of log, make loop about seven or eight inches in diameter, set small bush on each side, stick in log and cover just over top of snare. If properly set will catch fox, coon and dogs (so it is best to set where dogs do not travel).

I suppose any log up from the ground high enough would do by using the scent from the female fox. Another way, drive a stake beside a log, set trap about six to nine inches away, pour fish brine on stake and see what it will do. This should be away from dogs.

My way of trapping the fox is by the old method. Take a bushel of buckwheat chaff and where foxes travel nearly every night scatter it about four feet around, and take a stick and pat the chaff down so it is nice and smooth all over the bed. Then take tallow cracklings and scatter them over the bed about a foot apart, then leave everything natural, and as soon as a fox takes the bait place your trap (which should be a double spring Newhouse or a

No. 2 1/2 B. & L.) set it in center of bed and cover about 3/4 or 1 inch with chaff. Put cotton under pan so it will not hinder trap from springing. The trap should be fastened to a clog or drag hook. I say to young trappers try my way and you will be successful.

Do not spit or drop anything or touch anything with your bare hands, says a Vermont trapper. Yes, I know some say animals are not afraid of human scent. I have my ideas and know what I have to do to be successful. If others can make a success in a different way I will not disagree with them. You cut a stake, sharpen it at one end, cut it about 15 inches long, about 1 inch in diameter; leave a prong about three inches long and about three inches from top to stake down trap. I will set this No. 2 1/2 Blake now. I ask all of you to pay attention, as I have often made the assertion that I could set a fox trap before 400 persons and not ten of them would make fox trappers. Now let me set this trap and carry it set to this bank, which is a sharp knoll about two feet high. I take my digger and cut a sod 6 inches square. Now I dig a hole back in the bank 6 or 8 inches and about three inches across. Make the cavity large enough to set trap about 3 inches deep, place ring over stake and drive stake in ground under where you set the trap. Set trap so pan will be about three inches from mouth of hole and square in front of hole. Now with digger cover trap about 1/2 inch deep so it will be all covered evenly. Put two pieces of bait in hole beyond trap and about three inches from mouth, and one in further end of hole. Drop a few drops of scent at mouth of hole and the thing is done. If you have paid attention you will see that I have touched nothing with my hands and never stepped out of my tracks setting trap.

The fox is, without doubt, the most cunning of all cunning animals we trappers have to trap, says an Eastern trapper. Many times have I been to my fox traps to find one or so turned bottom side up and no fox. A fox will reach into a bed and take your bait with his paw, and I have trapped them when actions said plain as words, "you can't fool me."

I find the No. 1 1/2 Newhouse a very good trap for the fox, especially in early fall when the ground don't freeze. A fox will start on his nightly rounds and frequent small clearings in woods, sandy side hills and such places, and that is the place a trapper wants a few tanglefoot. I have trapped fox for quite a number of years, and I never caught one by accident yet. I always have to set for fox and fox only.

In regard to poisoning, I think that a man that uses it ought to be shot full of holes. In regard to iron smell, I will say that fox can smell iron, but bury your trap deep enough and you will be all right. A good scent is as follows: Take skunk essence, white of eggs, and let stand about one week. Use about five drops and I will warrant it to be the best fox scent made.

We all know it's difficult to catch the fox on dry land, although it is done, says a New England trapper. There are thousands of fox who fall victims to this way, and I believe it a more successful method than any in existence. I shall recommend a spring to set your trap in because the water does not rise or fall much, like a brook. Carefully dig out your spring in July or August, arranging it so that you will have it ready by fall, by placing a flat stone about fifteen inches from the stone so it will project above water about one inch; on top of this place a sod about three inches thick if possible, and have the edges come into the water so it will look natural. Cut your sods that you are to fix inside the trap, and lay up to dry when you prepare your place.

When the time is ready for setting your trap, go to the place by walking up the outlet of the spring or brook, using the greatest care, and not touch the brushes or anything around the trap; place your trap very near the edge of the spring, about six or eight inches from the sod; have the trap entirely under water, and place your sod, cut for the purpose, on the pan, have it cover all the space inside the trap, and be sure it is out of water enough to offer a dry footing for the fox, and not over two inches from the shore.

Some have the shore cut out so half the trap is on apparently dry land. Either way is all right. Place your bait on the side of the sod, using scent and being sure that your bait or scent cannot be reached except by the fox stepping on the pan of the trap, and you will get your fox.

When you visit your trap do not go too near, as all these things have their effect. I should recommend for bait cat or muskrat, a piece half the size of an egg is all right. It should be prepared by placing in a perfectly clean jar the number of bait you wish, and allow to taint, putting the scent in with the bait, or dropping on the bait after you place on sod. You must use the greatest care in handling your bait. Do not take out or place on the bait with your bare hands. Use a stick.

I have been waiting for some of the fox trappers of the Red River Valley, says a Minnesota trapper, to write and tell us how they manage to pinch Mr. Reynard's toes. I think we have a harder place here to trap fox than you Eastern fellows have. The country is just as level as a board and no timber, and we are liable to have a blizzard any hour. What makes it hard to trap is that the traps always blow in if you haven't got them in a good place. I have quite a trick to catch the fox, at least I have had the best luck with it. I first find a place where an old straw pile was burned, then smear my traps with blood and hide them good in ashes, erase all of my tracks and drop a few spirits of anise oil all around. For bait I generally use the entrails of a hog or beef. Last winter I caught two without any bait; just the oil. Last winter I had good luck with dead chickens. I always staple my traps to a clog of about twelve or fifteen pounds weight. On this clog I nailed the chicken and I got every fox that came around.

I only trapped one month with two traps, No. 2 Newhouse, and I got 6 fox and 1 wolf, and that was all the fox there were inside of about three or four miles, and I didn't have time to go further because I am a farmer and have my stock to tend.

If you know where there is a meadow with hay or straw stacked out on it, says Austin Palin, of

Indiana, and if you will go to this stack after a little snow and there has been a fox in the field, he will be pretty sure to have gone to the stack to nose around. I first go and catch some fish about 6 or 8 inches long. I generally get suckers. I now clean my traps by boiling them in weak lye, then reboil them in evergreen boughs. I think it advisable to run beeswax over your trap, but I have had success without the beeswax.

After you have your traps cleaned and fixed do not handle them with your bare hands but put on a pair of gloves, take your trap and fish and a piece of wood about 4 feet long and the thickness of your arm and go to the stack. Now raise up the edge of the hay at the ground and slip the fish (one will be enough) back under the hay 6 or 8 inches, then set your trap directly in front of it, covering with the fine chaff; now fasten the trap chain to the piece of wood and slip the stick back under the stack, working it around a little so when the fox gets fast he can pull it out easily. Now take a stick and straighten out the hay over the trap and scratch out all signs and your set is complete. Make the above set when there is no snow.

We trapped foxes by baiting in beds mostly, says a Michigan trapper, though we caught five in the following manner: A wounded deer had fallen near two down trees which lap with tops crossed. We drew the deer into the apex or pen, as we noticed that foxes had been visiting the carcass. We cut notches out of these trees which were old and moss-covered, and set traps in the places prepared, covering neatly with moss.

Foxes are prone to walk convenient logs investigating anything that attracts them, and rarely look for danger under foot if the trap has been well placed and cleverly hidden. We smoked our traps and handled them with mittens.

The red fox is the only species that abounds in this locality, says Wm. Muchon, of Minnesota. When run by the hounds he usually keeps half a mile ahead, regulating his speed by that of the hounds, occasionally pausing a moment to divert himself with a mouse or to contemplate the landscape or to listen for his pursuer.

A most spirited and exciting chase occurs when the dogs gets close upon one in the open field. The fox relies so confidently upon his superior speed that I imagine he half tempts the dog to the race, but if he be a smart dog, and their course lies down hill over smooth ground, Reynard must put his best foot forward and then sometimes suffers the ignominy of being run over by his pursuer, who, however, is quite unable to pick him up, owing to the speed. But uphill and in the woods the superior nimbleness and agility of the fox tells at once.

Carry the carcass of a pig or a fowl to a distant field in mid-winter, and in a few nights his tracks cover the snow about it. The inexperienced youth, misled by this seeming carelessness of Reynard, suddenly conceives a project to enrich himself with fur, and wonders why the idea has not occurred to him before and to others. I knew a youthful yeoman of this kind who imagined he had found a mine of wealth discovering on a remote side hill between two woods a dead porker, upon which it appeared all the foxes of the neighborhood did nightly banquet.

The clouds were burdened with snow and as the first flakes began to eddy down he set out, trap and broom in hand, already counting over in imagination the silver quarters he would receive for the first fox skin. With the utmost care and with a palpitating heart he removed enough of the trodden snow to allow the trap to sink below the surface. The next morning at dawn he was on his way to bring his fur. The snow had done its work effectually, and he believed had kept his secret well.

Approaching nearer, the surface was unbroken, and doubt usurped the place of certainty in his mind. A slight wound marked the side of the porker, but there was no footprint near it. Looking up the hill, he saw where Reynard had walked leisurely down toward his wanted bacon till within a few yards when he had wheeled, and with prodigious strides disappeared in the woods. The stream of silver quarters suddenly set in another direction.

The successful trapper commences in the fall, or before the first deep snow. In a field not too remote with an old axe he cuts a small place, say ten inches by fourteen in the frozen ground, and removes the earth to the depth of three or four inches, then fills the cavity with dry ashes in which are placed bits of roasted cheese. Reynard is very suspicious and gives the place a wide berth, but the cheese is savory and the cold severe. He ventures a little closer every night until he can reach and pick out a piece from the ashes, and finding a fresh supply of the delectable morsels every night is soon thrown off his guard and his suspicions lulled.

After a week of baiting in this way, the trapper carefully conceals his trap in the bed, first smoking it thoroughly with hemlock boughs so as to kill all smell of iron. If the weather favors, and the proper precautions have been taken he may succeed, though the chances are still greatly against him.

I will say that we keep four of the best fox traps in the shape of four hounds that can be found in our part of the country, writes J. A. McKinnon, of Canada, and as for the month of November we sold $85.00 worth of fur, it will be easily seen that they pay for their keep. The fox hound, like the coon dog, must be a good one, properly bred and trained for the purpose, and they are never first class until they are two or three years old, although I have killed foxes ahead of dogs that were only nine months old, but these turned out to be exceptionally good dogs, and out of a litter of six or eight puppies half of the number may be worthless for what I call a good fox hound is one that will hunt for his fox alone, and that will run all day if necessary.

I went out on the first snow and in one day captured three foxes, two of which I shot, and the other ran into a hollow log; he was running so hard I believe he would have got into the rail if there had been no hole at all. I also find that the morning is the best time to find a fresh track, as it is then that Reynard is up and taking his morning walk through the old barren meadows, and partly cleared fields, in search of mice and other small game.

In my experience I find that the females do not move around so much in the day time as the males do, for they are shyer than the males and are possessed of more cunningness. In our travels we always mark any fox dens we come across, so as to pay them a friendly call after a fresh fall of snow.

We use the Winchester repeating shot guns, and find that for long range and quick shooting they are the best. We sometimes use our rifles but a fox is a small mark to shot at if he is running at full speed. Brother trappers, get a pair of good fox hounds and you will get more foxes than with all the traps you could set in a week.

I don't think there are many men now living that have skinned many more fox than I have, yet I can learn every year something new about Reynard, says O. Douglass, of Michigan. But what I do want to know is this: I see so much about water sets, and I don't understand how it can be done only for the fun of it. I have bought for many years, and I have as yet to see many prime water trapped fox. They are caught too early to be prime, and I can't see where the money comes in to pay for your trouble.

Now trappers, don't you think it is better to make some fine dry land sets in July or August and bait them once a week until they are prime, and you have them coming to your beds and they are not afraid of your work? I say this to young trappers. I have been trying all ways for sixty years and have caught them many different ways, but I do think the water set is the poorest way of all. Dry land sets for me every time in November and December.

I make my beds early and I use the scrap from hog's lard. I take one skunk scent bag to each bed to draw them to the bait, and when they come once they will call again.

I see where a buyer was called to buy 14 fox hides and only found one prime skin. All water caught. That is my experience with water caught fox. They have to be caught too early. It may be different in some localities, but not here, as the water is frozen by the time fox are prime. Try dry land sets and see if I am not right, and have more money for your work later on.

I always set two traps to one bed, and cover with dry dirt until it freezes. Then I use chaff. Handle all with clean gloves and be as cunning as a fox yourself.

CHAPTER XV.

FRED AND THE OLD TRAPPER.

Young trappers can learn much by making the rounds with experienced trappers. The following conversation between Fred and an old Pennsylvania trapper is interesting:

"Where was the trap set? I do not see any bait pen."

"Fred, you take this stick and walk up slowly to him; go up close and give him a sharp blow across the back of the neck. That will fix him. You see that big mossy log laying on the bank over there. That was where he was caught. We will now set the trap again. See this little sink in the log. That is where the trap was set. This limb is what the trap was fastened to, one end on the ground and the other comes just up to the log where the trap is set, and we will staple the trap to it. We will now cover it with moss just like this on this log, but we will get it from another log. No one could tell that there was a trap there."

"Will not the fox smell it?"

"He might if it was not for this fox carcass. We will skin the fox. Look out there, Fred, do not disturb the moss or anything on that log where the trap is. Keep away from that. We will put this carcass in the little hollow and will drive a crotched stake straddle of its neck; drive it well down; now take this stick and rake some leaves over it, cover the neck where the stake is quite well, the rest of the carcass only lightly. You have done it very well and the fox will not notice what scent there is on the trap as long as that carcass is there."

"But you had no carcass there when you caught this one, and I have heard that a fox was afraid of the scent of iron."

"That is all bosh! Keep the traps free from all foreign scent and you need not be afraid of the scent of the iron, but if you catch some animal in the trap then you must have some of the scent of that animal around near the trap. This will overcome what scent there is on the trap. This, however, is only necessary with shy animals like the fox. Coon and skunk are not afraid of what they smell.

"How did you know that a fox would go on that log where that trap was set?"

"By knowing the nature of the animal. When the fox smelt the bear bait in the pen there we knew that he would get on the highest point near the pen to investigate, and that point was that log."

"Is this the only way you catch foxes?"

"No, this is only one of the many ways."

CHAPTER XVI.

EXPERIENCED TRAPPER'S TRICKS.

The fox is the most cunning animal we have, consequently he is the most difficult one to trap, says C. E. Matheny, of Ohio. But like all other animals he has a weak point, and if you attack him at this point he will, without a doubt, fall into your snares. One of the most important things when about to trap a fox is to have the trap perfectly clean. The word clean, in this sense, does not allude to freedom from rust, but means that the trap should be entirely free from human scent. In order to avoid this, the trap must be thoroughly washed in lye and when dry, well greased and smoked over burning feathers. It has already been said that the fox has a very keen scent, but it is particularly shy and scary at the least odor of the human body. It is therefore necessary when handling the trap to use clean buckskin, or still better, rubber gloves, and unless this important precaution is observed success is very improbable. The next step is to make the bed for the trap, and although there are various ways of doing this, the following, I believe, is the best method.

The bed should be about three and a half feet in diameter, and made of wheat, hay or buckwheat chaff. Some trappers use wood ashes, but any of the above will be found better. The ground upon which the bed is made should be hollowed out in the center so as to admit the trap, and the bed should be made as hard as possible and deep enough to cover the trap, and at the same time be perfectly level with the ground.

When the bed is made as directed, take the trap (which should be a No. 2 and have a chain and clog attached to it) and place it in the hollow in the center of the bed. After setting the trap put some of the chaff inside the jaws as high as the pan. Cover the pan with paper so that the chaff will not prevent its working freely, and then cover the whole with chaff and level it off so that the fox will not suspect a trap to be there; finally bait it with fresh meat, cheese, or better still, cracklings after lard is pressed out. Scatter them liberally over the bed; do not tramp about the bed more than is absolutely necessary, and cover up all foot-tracks as much as possible.

It is a good plan to smear the trap with assafoetida or melted beeswax, with a few drops of the oil of rhodium. These are all good and may be employed for the purpose of deceiving a particularly cunning fellow after all other stratagems fail. Another good plan is to bait the bed several times before setting the trap, until the fox begins to think that this is the best place it ever knew to find a choice morsel ready at all hours. When a proper degree of confidence appears to have been established then put the trap in its place and catch him--if you can.

First take a No. 3 Blake & Lamb trap, and look around over the fields or woods and find where the sand has washed down and is fine as wood ashes, says F. A. Aurand, of Michigan. You will always find if you keep close watch over the fields that a fox likes to get on the fine sand and play or walk over and around on it for some reason, as you will always find their tracks on the sand in the fall and spring. Now take for bait any of the following: dead chicken, or turkey, or beef's hind leg, but I think the best is beef's old head. Now take the old head, dig down in the sand and set the head down in the sand so that the jaws and nose are out of the sand about to the eyes. Now take your traps, about three No. 3 B. & L. traps, take a stake and fasten the rings to the stake, and drive the stake below the surface of the sand and cover it over the top.

Now dig a small trench for the chains, lay the chains in the trenches, a trench for each chain.

Spread the traps each way from the old head, and set the trap out away from the head as far as the chains will let them go, by driving the stake right close to the head. Then dig a small place in the sand so the trap will set just level with the surface of the sand, for each trap to set in. Take a small piece of cotton batton and put enough under each pan of the traps to keep the sand from getting under pans so they won't spring. Now take the sand that you took out of the places for the traps and cover them all over, traps, chains and all. Then take a small bush and brush out all your tracks and over the traps. If you have done your work well you can hardly tell where the traps are. You can use some good scent on the sand or on the old head, but I don't think it needs it. Fix the old head in the sand quite a little while before you want to trap. All I ever caught I caught in this way. If you do everything right I am sure of your success.

I have visited hundreds of trappers in Maine and Canada, and have learned many of the secrets of successful trapping from them and also from my own personal experience and observation, writes N. C. Burbank. I have come to the conclusion that the basis of all the most successful secret decoys for catching fox is the substance taken from the glands of the female fox during the running season, mixed with grease of some sort, together with contents of the glands of the skunk, preferably the female taken in the spring or latter part of the winter. I do not pretend to say that every one will be successful who uses that decoy. I am of the opinion, if directions are closely followed in the following method of water trapping for fox, you are reasonably sure to catch them if you use that decoy.

During the month of August or September select some spring or place about a foot and a half from the edge, or in the center of a circular spring that is not over 4 feet wide, a sod 8 or 10 inches across, and arrange a place to set the trap a few inches from the outside. This must be done early in the season, so all evidence of human work and scent will be removed before trapping time.

When the season arrives you are ready to set your trap, and you do so in the following manner: In selecting springs you must find one that has an outlet so you can walk in the water for a distance of three rods, six or eight is better. Set your trap and take it up to the spring or place selected, walking in the water and using the greatest care not to touch bushes or anything to leave the scent of yourself. Place the trap in the place prepared in the early season, being sure it is covered over entirely, chain and all, by water. Then cover with dead leaves or whatever is on the bottom of the spring. Place upon the trap pan a small sod as light a one as possible, allowing it to be out of the water at least one inch so that the fox in reaching for the bait will step on the sod, which should be six or eight inches from the shore. Fox, like the human being, do not like to wet their feet.

Now you have the trap set and then comes the baiting. Take a small piece of meat and place it on the larger sod, using great care not to leave human scent, take a few drops of this decoy and place on the bait. Also take a rotten stick and break off a piece 6 or 8 inches long, being careful of handling, and place two or three drops on the end and stick it into the sod so it will stick up two inches or such a matter above it. Your trap is now ready for Reynard, and if you use great care in setting and in visiting your traps I am certain of your success.

There are many methods of catching foxes and I am acquainted with them, not all, perhaps, as each man has a little different way, but I am satisfied the above for a water set it correct.

Here in the East where I am trapping near the mountains, if we could not catch fox on the snow path we would not get any prime fur, says J. H. Shufelt, of Canada.

I will give one of my snow sets that I use here for fox. It may not fit your case as every locality calls for its own method, and foxes are slyer in some places than others. I use a No. 3 Blake & Lamb trap with a three foot chain and grapple. How to fix the trap? I take a large kettle and fill with water and put my traps in and get the water boiling hot. For every dozen of traps I put in one-half pint of lime not air slacked, and boil for ten minutes. Now take out your traps, which will be odorless and white as snow, and use gloves in handling and setting them.

When you get ready to set your traps go out in a large field where foxes are traveling, make a good path across the field by traveling back and forth. Where you want to make a set leave a little partition across the path to guide the fox in the trap, which is covered with white paper and a little snow. Be careful in setting and not leave tracks outside of the path nor lay any sticks across. When going to your traps walk in the path, which makes it better, and don't let too much snow get over them. Be careful and you will get your fox.

Do foxes eat skunk? I might say in answer to this question they do, and they will kill skunk if found outside of their dens. And if a fox is run in a den where there is a skunk, their odor is most always sure to prove fatal to a fox in a very short time. Several instances of this kind have happened in this locality where I am hunting and trapping.

Foxes are very fond of skunk for food, and the musk makes a good scent for trapping foxes. A good scent for cold weather, for it never freezes. No doubt a good trapper will say, give me fresh bait. I might say give me a strong smelling bait, for when the fox is smelling a strong bait or scent he cannot smell anything else at the same time.

Now for instance, if you were going out for a fox hunt, and your hound got scented by skunk, it would spoil his scenting anything, and he could not follow the trail. Several experiences have led me to think this is one reason why we make a better catch on a damp or rainy night. The bait smells so much stronger that it takes up more of the game's sense of smell and makes our chance of a catch better. The old trapper will oftimes make this remark, "Boys, I am going to make a big catch tonight--why, because it is going to be a damp and rainy night." Who knows why?

I trap foxes by land and water set. I sometimes use a set called the all around land set. Every locality calls for its own method. I use two kinds of traps, Blake & Lamb and Newhouse. They are both all right. My trapping grounds are near the mountains where the foxes defy fox hounds, for they have dens in the rocks.

The Hunter-Trader-Trapper, Columbus, Ohio, is in touch with fox trappers, hunters and owners of hounds from all parts of America, so that interesting articles are constantly being received and published.

The following, by W. J. Taylor, of New York, is his method for trapping the red fox: Choose a rotten stump near their runways, cut out a cavity in the top of the stump deep enough to set trap and allow one-half inch of finely pulverized rotten wood to cover trap, spring and chain. Do not handle pulverized wood with your hands. Have your traps thoroughly greased, chain and all, then smoke with hemlock, spruce, cedar or pine boughs. Smoke until trap and chain are black. This is to stop the smell of steel. Sometimes I use a moss covered stump, that is a stump with moss growing all or partly around its sides. Cut the cavity the same in stump, cover lightly with pulverized rotten wood.

Now go to another moss covered stump, cut moss enough to cover top of stump, cut a circular piece out a little smaller than jaws of trap, place this right on top of trap, then place the rest on top of stump, trim outsides to match outside of stump. Handle moss with sharpened stick and knife, never with bare hands unless set is made one week before baiting and scenting. I generally make my sets two weeks before placing bait and scent.

Place bait about six or eight feet from stump, always on lower hillside. Daub your fox scent on top of stump, side towards your bait. For bait I use muskrat carcasses, skunk, dead hens, rabbits, fish or partly decomposed meat. My receipt for fox scent is fish oil one-half pint (made by placing fish in glass can in summer and hanging in sun until decomposed) the musk sacks of ten or more muskrats, one or more fox matrix which are obtained from the female fox, also fat from the inside of either sex is good. Mix all together. It will surely draw the fox.

CHAPTER XVII.

REYNARD OUTWITTED.

A good fox year can be counted upon with reasonable certainty once every five years, says Martin Hunter, on the Labrador coast, at least so say the oldest residents. The year before they begin to come down from the interior, then the climax for great numbers. Then the following year they decrease in numbers to what they were two years before, and the winter following so few that one or two about in miles of coast is a rarity.

Such was the case in the winter of 71; 69 had been a great fox year. What was not trapped in the winter of 70 had migrated back to the remote interior. Between the posts of Scum Islands and Moisie, a distance of twenty-one miles of coast, there was only known to be one fox--a red one--with a claw missing on his right paw, and he was as cunning an old fellow as ever bothered a trapper. For a night or two he would play all kinds of tricks down about Moisie, and then we would hear of him around Seven Islands. There being no kind of hunting, the people got anxious as to who would succeed in catching the old rascal.

Bait would be sprinkled about at certain places, and no traps. Big tail would come around and eat every scrap; this would be done for two or three nights in succession, and then the hunter would think the fox's fears were allayed, and carefully put two or three traps and the bait as usual. Next morning the bait would be gone, as before, but he would find his traps turned up side down.

The fox we will say would pass and repass at a certain up-turned root or a point of trees, then the hunter would think a trap in his beaten track would surely nip him. Not so, however. The trap would be nicely concealed, but old Reynard would deflex his road to suit the circumstances. Smoking, greasing, or all the usual modes of taking the smell from the iron traps were of no avail; when a trap was set where his supper was spread, that old fox would begin by digging a trench from a distance off in a straight line for the hidden traps, the closer he got to the danger the slower and more cautiously he would work. This we could see plainly next morning by standing outside his works and reading his signs.

There were better and older trappers in the field after this old stayer's life, but it was given to me to circumvent his maneuvers and possess his fur. I had reset my traps near the bait two nights in succession in the exact place where he had turned them over, and of course he burrowed along his old trench to get at them. This I carefully noted and set another trap in the trench on edge. Something told me I was going to be successful, and I hardly slept that night. I was on my snowshoes and off at the first grey of the February morning. Before I got to the point where my traps were set I saw his fresh tracks leading off in the same direction I was going. My heart beat with expectation and anticipation as I hurried forward; it was not for the value of the beast, but to have it to say I had killed the cunning fox of 1871 where all the old hunters had failed.

Yes there he was sure enough, as I turned the last point; I could hardly credit my good fortune, and was so afraid that he would even now escape that I walked right on top of him with my snowshoes. He was pinned down tight with my weight and was powerless to even wriggle. I slipped my left hand under the snowshoe and with my other hand pulled down his heart; a quiver or two and that fox was a good fox.

Indians never strike or shoot either foxes, mink or marten when they find them alive in the traps, as it causes the blood to collect and congeal where the blow was given, and spoils the looks of the skin, besides the annoyance of the blood when skinning. They hold the animal by the neck and with the other hand pull down the heart until the heart-strings break, and death is as sudden as if the spine were severed.

CHAPTER XVIII.

FOX SHOOTING.

The fox, although the cleverest animal sought after by New England hunters and trappers, says L. W. Beardsley, of Connecticut, seems to have one decided drawback, that of sight, which frequently costs him his life. Sly and clever with very acute nose and ear, he appears to be unable to tell a man from a tree or stone by sight alone, provided the person remains motionless, but the slightest motion is detected and sends him dusting for cover. The above I have proved to my entire satisfaction time and again when hunting this animal, a few instances of which I will quote below.

While walking along the tracks of the Berkshire Division R. R., which were bounded on the west by a steep hill with a fence three boards high, placed horizontally about eight inches apart skirting the track, I noticed beneath the lower board the legs of a fox moving toward me some seventy-five yards away. I stopped between the rails, half raising my 38-40 Stevens, telescope mounted, and waited for a favorable shot. When some thirty yards away the fox crawled under the fence and trotted down the bank immediately in front of me, where I stood in plain view. He stopped in the middle of the track and looked towards me unconcernedly for several seconds, then swung his head down the tracks in the direction of a train which was rapidly approaching from the south. This was my chance. I brought the cross hairs to bear just back of his foreleg and pulled. With one mighty bound in the air he fell back across the rails without a struggle, and I had to do some hustling to pull him out of the way before the train was upon us.

Again I was sitting on a stone, my back against a wall in an open pasture lot waiting in hopes a fox might use the runway which passed close by. I had been waiting quietly since 4 A. M. It was now 6:30, and I had nearly given up hopes of seeing a fox that morning and was getting perhaps rather careless about watching, when something rustled in the grass, and raising my eyes without moving my head, I saw a red fox in the act of passing in front of me not more than ten or fifteen feet away in the open lot.

I remained motionless until he was well past, then raising my gun slowly and carefully I fired at the back of his head as he was trotting leisurely away, all unconscious of my presence, and perhaps only saw twenty-five yards off. The fox never knew what had killed him, and I often wonder if that load of shot surprised him more than his sudden appearance surprised me, as I sat dozing on the rock. I used on this occasion a 10 ga. full choke Winchester, level action repeater Model 1901, loaded with 4 1/2 drs. black powder and 1 1/4 oz. B. shot.

Late one afternoon several years ago while out

hunting grey squirrel at Swamp Mortar Rock with Wm. E. Howes I, who was hunting about 200 yards south of "Bill," heard a fox barking just over a rise of ground, and cautiously approaching saw two foxes digging at the roots of a decayed stump. Just as I was getting within effective gun shot range I stepped on a twig which snapped with my weight. The sound started the animals. Neither saw me, however, as I had remained perfectly motionless. The moment the twig broke one took a course due east, the other quartered toward me disappearing in the thick laurels. There was a small opening in these bushes opposite me, and with cocked gun trained on this spot I waited the appearance of the fox.

In a moment he was in the clearing, and as he was stepping over a log about 30 yards away I gave him my right barrel and tumbled him over, and as he endeavored to get up I put on the finishing touches with my left. I was using a Baker full choke 28 in. 12 ga. loaded with 3 1/4 drs. black powder with 1 1/8 oz. No. 7 shot.

While looking for woodchuck signs early one spring on my way to pasture, I was following a old logging road when I saw a fox crossing in front of me and disappear in the ferns, going toward a high ledge west of the road. I stood still and waited. When the fox reached the lower part of the ledge he stopped about 75 or 80 yards from me and sat down. When his head was turned away I would sneak cautiously a few feet nearer, always standing motionless when he looked my way, and thus reduced the distance between us to about 50 yards.

At this point just as I was about to shoot the fox, who was partially concealed with leaves and ferns, moved some 10 yards up the ledge and was getting uneasy, although he had not seen me, and the wind was unfavorable for closer approach. I waited and he climbed nearly to the top of the ledge and laid down on a flat rock in the sun. With the utmost caution I slowly crawled back to the road and approached his foxship from the west, keeping some large rocks between us until I had approached within 35 yards. He was sitting up, breast toward me as I cautiously peeped over a rock, but his head was turned away, so I stepped out into plain view, leveling my gun as I did so. Slowly the fox turned his head and faced me, but he appeared to see nothing unusual in the silent figure clad in the worn gray hunting coat, brown overalls and soft brown hat.

I could see him twitch his ears and blink his eyes lazily in the glare of the setting sun. Fully a minute I stood admiring the picture. It seemed a pity to kill this clever fellow I had so easily outwitted. My eye dropped a little lower, the brass bead trembled on his breast, and through the faint haze of smokeless powder I saw the old quail thief kicking and struggling in the edge of the ledge. A moment later he toppled over his carcass, bounding from rock to rock in its 50 foot descent. I was using a 12 ga. full choke 30 in. Stevens, smokeless and B shot.

Another time I was sitting in the woods for grey squirrel early in October. It was about 5:30 A. M. and just getting light. I heard the tread of an animal behind me and the rustle of leaves, which ceased a few feet away. By rolling my eyes and slightly moving my head I could see the outlines of a fox standing behind me, hardly ten feet away. Cautiously I attempted to move the muzzle of my gun in his direction, but he detected me immediately and disappeared midst the laurels like a flash.

Although he had stood two or three minutes within a few feet of me before I attempted to turn evidently trying to figure out what I was, not until I had made a movement did he realize he was so near his old enemy, "man," which goes to show that Mr. Fox, with every other sense alert, is like many other of his wild brethren, unable to tell man from an inanimate by mere sight alone, when he remains motionless.

CHAPTER XIX.

A SHREWD FOX.

Several years ago, when foxes were more numerous here than they are now, the writer, R. B., of Canada, in company with two other hunters, went on a fox hunting expedition. We had two dogs which had not been trained but would follow a trail pretty well. We had to travel over newly-made ice a distance of three miles to a small island about a mile long and quite narrow, on which were three small groves of fir trees which was the only cover for game, the surface of the island being chiefly meadow and marsh land. We landed on the eastern end of the island, and within a short time after the hunt began one of the party shot a fox, and in the afternoon the writer got a chance at a shot and succeeded in knocking over a very fine red fox. As night was now near we started for home, intending to return next day and renew the hunt, as we knew there was yet another fox on the island. Next day, however, was stormy, and we postponed the hunt till the following day, which being fine gave us a good chance for our work.

The same party of hunters and dogs renewed the chase early in the morning but the fox seemed to have learned a lesson from the previous hunt, and all day long he was chased from grove to grove by the dogs without giving a chance of a shot at him. As night was fast approaching we began to fear our hunt was going to be unsuccessful when we discovered that the fox had changed his tactics, and instead of taking shelter in the groves had run clear out to one end of the island, which was very narrow, and as we thought would take to the ice and thus get away from us. However, we followed after him, and you may imagine our surprise when the fox, instead of going on the ice, suddenly turned around and came directly toward us, and when about one hundred yards distant suddenly disappeared as if the earth had swallowed him up; one of the party who knew there was an old uncovered well there shouted out, "the fox is in the well!" We all hastened to the spot, and sure enough there was Mr. Fox in the well clinging to some sticks floating in the water about eight feet below the surface of the ground. As we had no rope or any facilities for getting reynard out of the well alive, we had to take a mean and unsportsmanlike advantage of our prisoner by putting a small charge of shot into his head and then fishing him out of the water with a forked stick. That the fox could never have gotten out of the well by his own exertions I do not believe, but that he went into it to escape from us is certain.

CHAPTER XX.

STILL-HUNTING THE FOX.

Many have requested me to give my method of still-hunting the red fox. As my hair is turning gray and the red foxes are about all gone here I will give an outline of my method, and will try and not weary the reader with a long account, thus writes G. O. Green, of Illinois.

Winter is the best time for hunting the red fox, and I have been more successful in January and February than other months. There are always some localities where the red fox spends the day, curled up asleep, and it is generally in a hilly locality as far as he can get from the presence of man.

The still hunter has only to go to these places on fair days and hunt as far as possible against the wind. If the wind is blowing some so much the better--it will help to deaden the sound of the hunter's tread. When you get into likely ground walk slow, and be sure you observe every object on the ground, both in front and in fact at least three sides. The average still hunter hunts too fast and don't use his eyes in the right direction--if he is a bird hunter he will be looking up in the trees too much.

A red fox is a small animal, and the hunter must keep his eyes always on the ground while hunting the old Red. If snow is on the ground and the hunter jumps a fox without getting a shot, the hunter, if he is a novice, will be pretty sure to go on the run after the fox when he comes to the place where the fox has just jumped. When you find the fox has been jumped sit right down and eat your lunch, and wait twenty minutes or a half hour. The fox will run perhaps 80 rods then get on a log or stump and watch his back track, and if he does not see any one following him he will not go far before he will look for another place to lie down.

When you come to a place where the fox makes zigzag trail, stop and look very close in every direction for at least one hundred yards. The fox rarely makes a straight trail when he is going to lie down; in this he resembles the deer. The fox sleeps most soundly between 11 o'clock and 2 o'clock in the daytime, and I have killed most of mine during that time. A fox jumped after 3 o'clock in the afternoon will hardly lie down again that day. A double-barrel shotgun loaded with No. 4 shot will stop any fox up to about 50 yards; above that distance coarser shot usually straddle the fox. When the day is cold and snow is crusty, stay at home, for you will get no fox but plenty of exercise.

When a fox goes into the ground while you are trailing him, don't try to dig him out; it is hard work. On three occasions I have got his brush by going to the burrow about sundown and getting a good position near the burrow to wait for him to come out. I have never been disappointed in getting a shot about the time that you can see half a dozen stars twinkling. But it takes good eyes to see a fox in twilight.

Now reader, these are not all the points of still hunting. It takes a peculiar cuss for a still hunter, and still hunters are born that way; all the education in the world will not make a still hunter.

CHAPTER XXI.

FOX RANCHES.

It is estimated that at present nearly 50 of the Aleutian Islands have fox ranches, most of which are said to have been successfully managed. Thus far the Government has rented the islands for this purpose at $100 per year. Some years ago the revenue cutter Perry was sent to the Archipelago by the Treasury Department for the express purpose of ascertaining the location of the islands used for fox ranches. The Government's agents were not long in finding out that in several instances the fox raisers had appropriated islands for which they were paying no rental. These persons were brought up with a sharp turn and ordered to pay up or shut up shop.

It seems quite clear that where proper business methods have been followed the ranches, without exception, have succeeded thus far, and will prove immensely valuable in the future. On some of the islands the work has been going on for 12 or 15 years, and three of them now have a fox population of more than 1,000 each. The first method was to begin operations by turning loose on an island several pairs of foxes. In some instances the animals have increased rapidly, with the result that in a year or so it had become apparent that $150 or $200 paid for a pair of mated animals was likely to prove a good investment.

The original project was to breed the silver gray fox, as the fur of this animal is much more valuable than that of the commoner varieties. A good silver gray pelt is worth about $50 to the original seller, while $15 or thereabout is the price for the pelt of the blue fox. But the silver gray has many peculiarities which make its domestication exceedingly difficult, practically impossible, in fact. It is much given to devouring its young, and it has many of the characteristics of the wolf. At present only one of the islands is given up to the silver grays, and the animals do not increase rapidly.

The blue fox, so called, is handled much more successfully. It is readily tamed, and if kindly treated soon becomes so domestic that it will take food from the keeper's hand. The food usually is fish, either cooked or raw, and a mixture of corn meal and tallow. Reynard gets these rations, and all he wants of them, for ten months in the year, the food being supplied steadily except during the two midsummer months. It is estimated that the average cost of the rations is $1.50 per fox per year. There are two or three keepers for each ranch who devote all their time the year around to their charges.

From November 20 to January 20 is the open season for foxes on the islands, and box traps, rather than dead falls or steel traps, are used. This is done because all the female animals are released, after having been marked, and also one male for every six of the opposite sex. The average age for killing is about 18 months, although the pelt of an animal eight months old is fully developed, and, despite some theories to the contrary, the fur does not necessarily improve with age. On some of the larger farms, the box trap method of catching the foxes has been given up, as being too slow, for baiting the animals near a small corral.

During the months preceding the killing time, the food for the foxes is placed near the site of this corral, in order to accustom the animals to coming to that locality, and also in order to tame them. Under this treatment the foxes lose their shyness and shrewdness to such an extent that they not only enter the corral freely, but the female or male which has once been released after having been examined and marked, frequently enters the corral again. It is reported that in some instances the same animal has been caught three or four times in the same night.

CHAPTER XXII.

STEEL TRAPS.

In sections the larger game is gone yet there is in parts of the North, West and South much good trapping territory that will pay the hardy trappers for years to come. Even in the more thickly settled districts trapping can be made a good paying business. It seems that red fox, skunk and muskrat remain about as numerous in most sections as ever. In fact, the red fox in certain sections has only made its appearance of late years--since the country has become more thickly settled. Trappers in most sections can rest assured that they will have game to trap for years to come.

In the rapid development of the country the steel trap has played a wonderful part. They have subdued the monster bear and have as well caught millions of the small fur bearing animals, adding largely to the annual income of the hardy trapper. Steel traps have been in use for more than fifty years, but for many years after they were invented they were so expensive that they were not generally used. Of late years they have become cheaper and their use has become general. In fact, the price is now so reasonable that the trapper, on his first expedition, has a supply. The professional trapper, who in the North, spends from seven to nine months in the woods has a supply of these traps, ranging from the smallest to the largest. His needs are such too that all of them are in use during the trapping season. A trapper can use from 50 to 250 traps.

Traps are made in various sizes. The smallest No. 0 is used for gophers, rats, etc., while the largest, No. 6, is for the grizzly bear and will hold him. The No. 2 is known as the fox trap having two springs and spread of jaws of 4 7/8 inches. The No. 1 1/2 single spring is also much used by fox trappers. The No. 1 will also hold the fox, but we think best to use the No. 1 1/2 or No. 2.

We are alluding to the Newhouse manufactured by the Oneida Community, Ltd., Oneida, N. Y., as it is acknowledged to be the best trap in the world.

As most fox trappers devote more or less time to trapping other fur bearing animals, a description of the various Newhouse traps, telling the animal or animals each size is adapted to, etc., will no doubt be of Interest.

Spread of Jaws, 3 1/2 inches. This, the smallest trap made, is used mostly for catching the gopher, a little animal which is very troublesome to western farmers, and also rats and other vermin. It has a sharp grip and will hold larger game, but should not be overtaxed.

Spread of Jaws, 4 inches. This Trap is used for catching muskrats and other small animals, and sold in greater numbers than any other size. Its use is well understood by professional trappers and it is the most serviceable size for catching skunks, weasels, rats and such other animals as visit poultry houses and barns.

Spread of Jaws, 4 inches. Occasionally animals free

themselves from traps by gnawing their legs off just below the trap jaws, where the flesh is numb from pressure. Various forms of traps have been experimented with to obviate this difficulty. The Webbed Jaws shown above have proved very successful in this respect.

Noting the cross-section of the jaws, as illustrated at the left, it is plain the animal can only gnaw off its leg at a point quite a distance below the meeting edges. The flesh above the point of amputation and below the jaws will swell and make it impossible to pull the leg stump out of the trap.

The No. 81 Trap corresponds in size with the regular No. 1 Newhouse.

Spread of Jaws--#91, 5 1/4 inches; #91 1/2, 6 1/4 inches. The double jaws take an easy and firm grip so high up on the muskrat that he can not twist out. A skunk cannot gnaw out either.

These traps are especially good for Muskrat, Mink, Skunk and Raccoon.

All parts of the No. 91 except the jaws are the same size as the regular No. 1 Newhouse, while the 91 1/2 corresponds to the regular No. 1 1/2.

Spread of Jaws, 4 7/8 inches. This size is called the Mink Trap. It is, however, suitable for catching the Woodchuck, Skunk, etc. Professional trappers often use it for catching Foxes. It is very convenient in form and is strong and reliable.

Spread of Jaws, 4 7/8 inches. The No. 2 Trap is called the Fox Trap. Its spread of jaws is the same as the No. 1 1/2 but having two springs it is, of course, much stronger.

Spread of Jaws, 5 1/2 inches. This, the Otter Trap, is very powerful. It will hold almost any game smaller than a bear.

Spread of Jaws, 6 1/2 inches. This is the regular form of Beaver Trap. It is longer than the No. 3 Trap, and has one inch greater spread of jaws. It is a favorite with those who trap and hunt for a living in the Northwest and Canada. It is also extensively used for trapping the smaller Wolves and Coyotes in the western stock raising regions.

Spread of Jaws, 6 1/2 inches. In some localities the Otter grows to an unusual size, with great proportionate strength, so that the manufacturers have been led to produce an especially large and strong pattern. All the parts are heavier than the No. 2 1/2, the spread of jaws greater and the spring stiffer.

Spread of Jaws, 5 inches. The above cut represents a Single Spring Otter Trap. It is used more especially for catching Otter on their "slides." For this purpose a thin, raised plate of steel is adjusted to the pan so that when the trap is set the plate will be a trifle higher than the teeth on the jaws. The spring is very powerful, being the same as used on the No. 4 Newhouse Trap. The raised plate can be readily detached if desired, making the trap one of general utility.

Single Spring. Same as No. 2 1/2 but without Teeth or Raised Plate.

No. 31 1/2 NEWHOUSE TRAP.

Single Spring. Same as No. 3 1/2 but without Teeth or Raised Plate.

Spread of Jaws--No. 21 1/2, 5 1/4 inches; No. 31 1/2, 6 1/2 inches. These Traps are the largest smooth jaw, single spring sizes that are made. Professional trappers will find these especially valuable when on a long trapping line, as they are more compact and easier to secrete than the large double spring traps. The springs are made extra heavy.

Note.--The 21 1/2 is practically a single spring No. 3 and the 31 1/2 a single spring No. 4.

Spread of Jaws, 6 1/2 inches. This Trap is the same in size as the No. 4 Beaver, but has heavier and stiffer springs and offset jaws, which allow the springs to raise higher when the animal's leg is in the trap, and is furnished with teeth sufficiently close to prevent the animal from pulling its foot out.

Clutch Detachable--Trap can be used with or without it.

PATENTED.

Spread of Jaws, No. 23, 5 1/2 inches; No. 24, 6 1/4 inches. The inventor of this attachment claims to have had wonderful success with it in taking Beaver. The trap should be set with the clutch end farthest from shore. The beaver swims with his fore legs folded back against his body, and when he feels his breast touch the bank he puts them down. The position of the trap can be so calculated that he will put his fore legs in the trap, when the clutch will seize him across the body and hold him securely.

In response to a demand for a new model of the Newhouse Trap especially adapted to catching wolves, the manufacturers have perfected a trap which is numbered 4 1/2 and is called the "Newhouse Wolf Trap."

This trap has eight inches spread of jaw, with other parts in proportion, and is provided with a pronged "drag," a heavy snap and an extra heavy steel swivel and chain, five feet long, warranted to hold 2,000 pounds. The trap complete with chain and "drag" weighs about nine pounds.

Spread of Jaws, 9 inches. This trap is intended for catching small sized Bears. In design it is exactly like the standard No. 5 Bear Trap, only that the parts are all somewhat smaller. Weight, 11 1/4 pounds each.

Spread of Jaws, 9 inches. This trap is identical with No. 5 excepting that the jaws are offset, making a space five-eighths inch between them. This allows the springs to come up higher when the bear's foot is in the trap, and thus secure a better grip. Also there is less chance of breaking the bones of the foot. Weight, 11 1/4 pounds each.

Spread of Jaws, 11 3/4 inches. This trap weighs nineteen pounds. It is used for taking the common Black Bear and is furnished with a very strong chain.

Spread of Jaws, 11 3/4 inches. To meet the views of certain hunters whose judgment is respected, the manufacturers designed a style of jaw for the No. 5 trap, making an offset of 3/4 of an inch, so as to allow the springs to come up higher when the bear's leg is in the trap. This gives the spring a better grip. Those wishing this style should specify "No. 15."

Spread of Jaws, 16 inches. Weight, complete, 42 pounds. This is the strongest trap made. We have never heard of anything getting out of it when once caught. It is used to catch lions and tigers, as well as the great Grizzly Bears of the Rocky Mountains.

This cut illustrates Bear Chain Clevis and Bolt, intended as a substitute for the ring on the end of the trap chain, when desired.

With this clevis a loop can be made around any small log or tree without the trouble of cutting to fit the ring. The chain is made five feet long, suitable for any clog, and the prices of bear traps fitted with it are the same as with the regular short chain and ring.

Every trapper knows how difficult it is to set a large trap alone in the woods, especially in cold weather, when the fingers are stiff, and the difficulty is greatly increased when one has to work in a boat. One of these clamps applied to each spring will, by a few turns of the thumb-screws, bend the springs to their places, so that the pan may be adjusted without difficulty. No. 4 Clamp can be used on any trap smaller than No. 4 1 /2. No. 5 and 6 are strong clamps, carefully made and especially adapted to setting the large traps Nos. 4 1/2 to 6. They dispense with the inconvenient and dangerous use of levers. With them one can easily set these powerful traps. These clamps are also useful about camp for other purposes.

Printed in Great Britain
by Amazon